AFRICAN AMERICAN CHRONOLOGY

AFRICAN AMERICAN REFERENCE LIBRARY

AFRICAN AMERICAN CHRONOLOGY

VOLUME 1
1492-1972

by Alton Hornsby, Jr. and Deborah Gillan Straub

An Imprint of Gale Research Inc.

*A*FRICAN AMERICAN *A*CHRONOLOGY

Alton Hornsby, Jr., and Deborah Gillan Straub, Editors

STAFF

Carol DeKane Nagel, *U•X•L Developmental Editor*
Thomas L. Romig, *U•X•L Publisher*

Amy Marcaccio, *Acquisitions Editor*

Shanna P. Heilveil, *Production Assistant*
Evi Seoud, *Assistant Production Manager*
Mary Beth Trimper, *Production Director*

Cynthia Baldwin, *Art Director*
Arthur Chartow, *Technical Design Services Manager*

Weigl Educational Publishers Limited, *Page and Cover Design and Typesetting*

This book is printed on acid-free paper that meets the minimum requirements of American National Standard for Information Sciences—Permanence Paper for Printed Library Materials, ANSI Z39.48-1984.

ISBN 0-8103-9231-3 (Set)
ISBN 0-8103-9232-1 (Volume 1)

Printed in the United States of America

Published simultaneously in the United Kingdom
by Gale Research International Limited
(An affiliated company of Gale Research Inc.)

I(T)P™

The trademark **ITP** is used under license.

AFRICAN AMERICAN REFERENCE LIBRARY

AFRICAN AMERICAN REFERENCE LIBRARY

The **African American Reference Library** fills the need for a comprehensive, curriculum-related reference covering all aspects of African American life and culture. Aimed primarily at middle school and junior high school students, this nine-volume set combines appropriate reading level and fascinating subject matter with quality biographies, statistics, essays, chronologies, document and speech excerpts, and more.

The **African American Reference Library** consists of three separate components:

African American Chronology (two volumes) explores significant social, political, economic, cultural, and educational milestones in black history. Arranged by year and then by month and day, this work spans from 1492, when sailor Pedro Alonzo Niño arrived in the new world with explorer Christopher Columbus, until June 30, 1993, when Los Angeles, California, mayor Tom Bradley stepped down from office after twenty years of service. The *Chronology* features 106 illustrations and maps, extensive cross references directing the reader to related entries, and a cumulative subject index providing easy access to the events and people discussed throughout the volumes.

African American Biography (four Volumes) profiles three hundred African Americans, both living and deceased, prominent in their fields, from civil rights to athletics, politics to literature, entertainment to science, religion to the military. A black-and-white portrait accompanies each entry, and a cumulative subject index lists all individuals by field of endeavor.

African American Almanac (three volumes) provides a comprehensive range of historical and current information on African American life and culture. Organized by subject, the volumes contain 270 black-and-white illustrations, a selected bibliography, and a cumulative subject index.

Comments and suggestions

We welcome your comments on *African American Chronology* as well as your suggestions for topics to be featured in future **African American Reference Library** series. Please write:

Editors, **African American Reference Library**, U•X•L, 835 Penobscot Bldg., Detroit, Michigan 48226-4094; or call toll-free: 1-800-877-4253.

CONTENTS

INTRODUCTION

Out of Africa (300-1619)

The ancestors of most black Americans came from the area of the African continent known as the Western Sudan. This area stretched from the Atlantic Ocean in the west to Lake Chad in the east, and from the Sahara Desert in the north to the Gulf of Guinea in the south.

From about 300 A.D. to the late 1500s, three different empires ruled the Western Sudan. The first was Ghana, followed by Mali and later Songhai. All three grew rich and powerful through trade with their Arab neighbors to the north. The Arabs in turn brought the teachings of Muhammad to the Western Sudan during the seventh and eighth centuries, and Islam soon became an important cultural force.

Under the leadership of Askia Muhammad Touré, whose rule began in 1492, the Western Sudan became the largest and richest country in Africa. Askia Muhammad established an efficient system of centralized government and hired Arab scholars to teach in his empire's two major universities. One of them was located in the city of Timbuktu. It was known throughout the Muslim world as a major center of learning and trade.

In 1528, Askia Muhammad's sons forced their elderly father to give up his throne. For more than fifty years, the brothers fought over who would be in charge as the empire grew weaker and weaker. Finally, in 1590 an invading army from Morocco crushed what was left of the last great black kingdom of West Africa.

The people of West Africa passed along to their descendants a rich tradition of economic success, self-government, religious worship, and cultural expression through music, dance, art, and storytelling. But they also left behind a legacy of slavery. In ancient times, West Africans sold their slaves (many of whom were prisoners of war) to Arab traders. By the early 1500s, however, the West Africans were selling or trading other Africans to Europeans for cloth, rum, and weapons. Portuguese and Spanish colonists then used these slaves on their sugar plantations in Brazil and the West Indies. After 1600, England, France, and the Netherlands also began using slaves in their colonies in North America. Blacks were enslaved in other ways, too. Some were captured by traders in Africa or kidnapped from ships.

Slave voyages across the Atlantic Ocean usually took several months. Since selling more slaves meant making more money, traders and ship captains tried to deliver as many slaves as possible. Conditions on board the boats were horribly crowded and dirty. Except for brief exercise periods, slaves were generally chained together below deck all day and night. Sickness and death were very common. In fact, historians believe that about 12 percent of all slaves died during the Atlantic crossings.

ix

The slave trade between Europe and the Americas lasted until the 1800s. Although the exact number of Africans who were sold into slavery is unknown, the most reliable estimates range from 10,000,000 to 20,000,000. Between 400,000 and 1,200,000 of these people were brought to North America. It was there that they began the long cultural process of becoming African Americans.

Indentured Servants and Slaves (1619-1860)

Blacks were part of the early expeditions to the New World, perhaps even the first voyage of Christopher Columbus. But the first permanent settlers in what would one day be the United States were the twenty blacks dropped off at Jamestown, Virginia, in 1619. Captured in Africa and sold to the highest bidders, they were indentured servants rather than slaves. (Many lower-class whites were kidnapped and forced to suffer the same fate.) As indentured servants, they had to work for someone for a specific period of time, usually seven years. After their term of service ended, some of these free blacks became property owners and community leaders.

African Americans probably lived as indentured servants in the American colonies as late as the mid-1600s. Their total number was very small, however—only about 300 servants, slaves, and free blacks by 1650. But by the time of the American Revolution in 1776, there were about half a million black slaves in the colonies. Almost half of the population in several southern states, including Virginia and Maryland, was black. In South Carolina, blacks outnumbered whites. About 16,000 slaves lived in the North, where Connecticut was the leading New England slave colony. Unlike indentured servants, slaves belonged to their owners, just like farm animals or household goods.

In the South, most slaves helped plant and harvest crops. The typical slave worked on a small farm with one or two other blacks alongside the master and his family. Other slaves worked in and around the master's house instead of out in the fields. In towns and cities, blacks served as messengers, house servants, and craftsmen.

In the North, farming was not as important to the economy as it was in the South. Black slaves therefore worked in a wider variety of jobs. They provided skilled and unskilled labor in homes, ships, factories, and shipyards.

Since England had no laws that defined the status of a slave, the colonies made up their own. These "slave codes" protected the property rights of the master. They also made sure white society was guarded against what was considered a strange and savage race of people. Slaves had almost no rights of their own.

Enforcement of the slave codes varied from one area to another, and even from one plantation to another. Slaves who lived in cities and towns were less restricted than slaves who lived in the country, and slaves on small farms enjoyed more freedom than those on huge plantations. It was on some of the larger plantations that blacks who disobeyed or who tried to run away faced cruel punishments.

Despite the risks, some blacks constantly tried to undermine the slavery system. A few chose rather minor ways, including destroying property and faking illness to avoid having to work. Others took bolder steps to overthrow their masters by joining slave revolts. Still others managed to escape. But many—perhaps most—slaves chose not to resist in the face of almost certain failure and even death.

A few slaves won their freedom, especially in the years just after the Revolutionary War. In appreciation for the service of about 5,000 blacks in the colonists' struggle against the British, and in the spirit of liberty and equality inspired by the Declaration of Independence, many masters (especially in the North) freed their slaves. Soon individual states in the North began making slavery illegal. Statesmen such as George Washington and Thomas Jefferson predicted that slavery would eventually disappear from the land as more and more blacks were freed by law or by their masters.

In the rural South, these free blacks did farm work for others or became independent farmers. In urban areas of the North and South, they were factory workers, businessmen, preachers, craftsmen, and personal servants. Many became successful and prosperous. It was not long, however, before some whites grew frightened by the rapid increase in the population of free blacks. Beginning around 1790, several states passed laws restricting free blacks that left them little better off than slaves.

In 1793, a machine patented by Eli Whitney of Massachusetts changed the course of American history, especially for blacks. His invention, called the cotton gin, separated the cotton from the seeds, hull, and other material. Suddenly, raising cotton became much more profitable for southern farmers. As a result, the number of slaves grew from about half a million in 1776 to four million in 1860, just before the outbreak of the American Civil War.

War, Freedom, and Reconstruction (1861-1876)

The Civil War began on April 12, 1861, following an attack by southern troops on Fort Sumter, South Carolina. In the months just before the first cannons were fired, seven states had seceded, or broken away, from the Union. Led by South Carolina, with Mississippi, Florida, Alabama, Georgia, Louisiana, and Texas following soon after, they formed the Confederate States of America.

The disagreements between the North and the South dated back many years. They grew out of a variety of economic and political rivalries and issues, including whether a state had the right to secede from the Union. Slavery was also a source of conflict, but the Civil War was not a war against slavery. President Abraham Lincoln had made it clear that he had no intention of interfering with slavery where it already existed, and he did not approve of blacks fighting in the Union Army. He was, however, determined to keep the Union together.

The first year of the Civil War went badly for the North. The abolitionists (a group of militant reformers who were demanding freedom for black slaves) refused to support a war whose goals did not include ending slavery and allowing black soldiers to serve in combat. By the summer of 1862, President Lincoln realized he had to change his policies or risk defeat. So, on September 22, 1862, he took a major step that he hoped would give a much-needed boost to the Union effort: he issued the Emancipation Proclamation. Effective on January 1, 1863, it declared slaves free in all states and territories then at war with the United States and opened the door for blacks to serve in the Union Army.

About 200,000 blacks ended up fighting for the Union during the Civil War. Although they faced discrimination at every turn, many served with honor (a few became officers) and were even singled out for praise from the president himself. Around 40,000 black troops lost their lives, mostly from disease.

The war finally came to an end on April 9, 1865, when Confederate General Robert E. Lee surrendered to Union General Ulysses S. Grant near the Appomattox Courthouse in Virginia. President Lincoln and most other white northerners were eager to put the country back together again as soon as possible. His plans to reorganize and rebuild the defeated South, a program known as Reconstruction, were especially generous and lenient. But less than a week after the war ended, Lincoln was assassinated. His successor, Andrew Johnson, was a southerner who promised to continue Lincoln's policies in the spirit of reconciliation. But even though President Johnson supported outlawing slavery, he made little effort to grant blacks civil rights protection or give them the vote. He tolerated anti-black violence in some southern states, and he did nothing to stop white governments in the South from passing laws similar to the old slave codes.

Republican leaders in Congress were afraid that President Johnson was just making it easier for white Democrats to gain control once again throughout the South. So they came up with a much harsher Reconstruction program. Under their plan, the southern states would not be allowed to rejoin the Union until the Republicans had become stronger and until blacks were given the vote and guaranteed civil rights.

In 1866 and 1867, the Republicans took over the Reconstruction effort from President Johnson and began pushing their radical reforms through the House of Representatives and the Senate. In 1870, for example, the Fifteenth Amendment to the Constitution was ratified, or approved, and blacks were finally granted the right to vote. For the first time, they participated in large numbers in southern politics, electing members of their own race and sympathetic whites to offices ranging from city councilman to U.S. senator.

The Spirit of Reconstruction Fades (1877-1900)

By the mid-1870s, the Republicans had begun to lose interest in radical Reconstruction efforts. Their presence in the South came to an end for the most part following the presidential election of 1876. In this controversial contest, southern Democrats agreed to certify Republican candidate

Rutherford Hayes as president if the Republicans promised two things. First of all, they had to give more federal aid to the South. Secondly, they had to withdraw the federal troops who were still stationed in the South to enforce Reconstruction policies. The Republicans accepted the Democrats' conditions, and Hayes became president.

The next two decades were among the darkest years in African American history. Abandoned by the Republican party and stripped of the protection of federal troops, blacks now had to deal on their own with southern whites who acted quickly to take control again. One state after another legalized segregation and discrimination, even passing laws making it almost impossible for blacks to vote. In a series of decisions during the 1880s and 1890s, the U.S. Supreme Court upheld these new laws and struck down older ones that had guaranteed blacks certain civil rights.

Meanwhile, the national government followed a "hands-off" policy toward the South. It was not long before blacks were living under conditions very similar to those they had known under slavery. Making matters even worse was a rise in violence against blacks, especially lynching. But out of this grim atmosphere came two new leaders who would have a major impact on African American history—Booker T. Washington and W.E.B. Du Bois.

The Age of Booker T. Washington (1901-1917)

As the founder and head of Alabama's Tuskegee Institute, Booker T. Washington was already famous when he spoke at the 1895 Cotton States International Exposition in Atlanta, Georgia. In his speech, which came to be known as the "Atlanta Compromise," he advised blacks to stop demanding political power and social equality. Instead, he asked whites to help blacks advance economically through education, primarily in the areas of agriculture and industrial arts. Once blacks showed how much they could contribute to the American economy, Washington reasoned, whites would grant equality to blacks out of respect and gratitude.

This formula for racial peace and progress received widespread approval among whites in the North as well as the South. Many blacks also supported it. But others strongly disagreed with Washington and his "accommodationist" ideas, which expected blacks to accept things the way they were and wait patiently for change.

One of Washington's harshest critics was scholar W.E.B. Du Bois. In mid-1905, a group of black "radicals" led by Du Bois and publisher William Monroe Trotter met at Niagara Falls, Canada. There they called for immediate and aggressive action to end racial discrimination in the United States. The group held other meetings throughout America and added members from nearly every major city.

In 1909, following anti-black riots in Texas, Georgia, and Illinois, the so-called "Niagara Movement" merged with a group of white liberals to form the National Association for the Advancement of Colored People (NAACP). Its goal was to obtain racial equality for all Americans.

Soon it had earned a reputation as the most militant civil rights organization in the United States.

Despite the efforts of the Niagara Movement and the NAACP, Booker T. Washington remained very popular among most blacks, wealthy whites, and national and local political figures. But after his death in 1915, there was no one person powerful enough or respected enough to take his place as the spokesman for black America. So several different people, including some members of the NAACP, shared the leadership role.

Between War and Depression (1918-1932)

For the most part, white Americans opposed the demands of these new black leaders. Racial oppression continued, including police brutality, lynchings, and legal discrimination in employment, housing, education, and voting. Even black soldiers who served during World War I experienced harassment at home and overseas. After the war, during the summer of 1919, the United States was rocked by some of the worst race riots in the country's history.

The 1920s were a time of disappointment and despair for black Americans. Yet it was also a decade of great creativity and energy. In New York City's Harlem, for example, a group of black writers and artists began producing works that showed the realities of ghetto life and cried out for relief from oppression. (The movement came to be known as the "Harlem Renaissance.") Across the rest of the country, black singers, musicians, and composers entertained audiences with their talents.

Meanwhile, West Indian immigrant Marcus Garvey appealed to quite a few dissatisfied blacks with a revival of black nationalism. He stressed race pride and urged his followers to return to Africa. Garvey's dream of establishing a new empire faded when he went to prison for mail fraud.

The Great Depression that hit the United States in 1929 was especially hard on blacks, most of whom were already struggling to make a living. Discrimination made their suffering even worse. When Franklin Roosevelt took office as president in 1933, American blacks were more than ready for the "New Deal" he had promised to those who voted for him.

A New Deal—A New Life? (1933-1940)

President Roosevelt's various recovery and reform programs—such as the Civilian Conservation Corps (CCC), the National Youth Administration (NYA), and the Works Progress Administration (WPA)—helped blacks as well as whites. But because many of them were supervised by whites at the state and local level, blacks could not help but wonder if they were receiving their fair share of benefits, especially in the South. Nevertheless, they welcomed the New Deal as a sign of hope and progress.

There were other reasons for optimism, too. Although President Roosevelt relied primarily on white advisors, he also turned to a group that came to be known as his "Black Cabinet." Among its members were prominent blacks in a variety of fields, including educator Mary McLeod Bethune and political scientist Ralph Bunche. They kept the president informed about issues of interest to African Americans.

War Again (1941-1945)

In 1939, the outbreak of World War II in Europe sent many southern blacks north in search of good-paying factory jobs. But discrimination shut them out of many companies. Finally, after blacks threatened to march in protest on Washington, D.C., President Roosevelt issued an order forbidding discrimination in defense-related industries.

Once the United States entered the war in 1941, hundreds of thousands of black Americans served in the armed forces. Their distinguished role in the victory, along with the growing black population in American cities, a rise in the literacy rate among blacks, and increasing economic opportunities, inspired new efforts to end racial discrimination. Leading the way was the NAACP.

The Attack against Segregation (1945-1953)

Basing their arguments on rights guaranteed in the Constitution, NAACP lawyers began challenging segregation and discrimination in the courts. They took many of their cases all the way to the U.S. Supreme Court, winning several important decisions before the war. But the big push came after the war, when the NAACP slowly but surely demolished legalized segregation and discrimination in all areas of American life—voting, housing, transportation, education, and recreation, to name just a few. The Supreme Court's decisions on school segregation, including the landmark *Brown v. Board of Education* in 1954, were especially important. They brought about changes that launched a whole new era in African American history, the era of civil rights.

"The Second Reconstruction" (1954-1964)

As the courts destroyed what remained of legalized segregation, other branches of government took action, too. Congress passed laws to make sure white southerners could not cheat blacks out of their right to vote. President Harry S. Truman banned segregation in the armed forces. Later, President Dwight Eisenhower ended discrimination in federal housing assistance programs. In addition, civil rights committees assembled to investigate and report on injustices.

Even though segregation and discrimination were against the law, they had not just disappeared. So blacks turned their attention to fighting the kind of bias that was common in restaurants and hotels, on buses, and in other public places. Boycotts and sit-ins became popular and effective ways to protest. In fact, blacks achieved so much in the area of civil rights from 1954 until 1964 that some people started to think of the decade as "The Second Reconstruction." To them, the work of the first Reconstruction after the Civil War had been left unfinished, and now was the time for it to continue.

"The Second Reconstruction" Fades (1964-1973)

The landmark Civil Rights Law of 1964 had barely gone into effect when a serious race riot erupted in Harlem. Racial disturbances occurred that summer in several other northern ghettos. A year later, during the summer of 1965, the black ghetto of Watts in Los Angeles, California, exploded in violence. For the next two summers, dozens of other riots broke out across the country. Many were sparked by fights between blacks and white police officers.

A special presidential commission looked into the reasons behind the riots. Its members found that despite all of the court decisions, sit-ins, marches, and boycotts, the average black American was still living with the crippling effects of segregation, discrimination, and, above all, racism. The 1968 assassination of civil rights leader Martin Luther King, Jr.—a champion of nonviolence—added to the sense of despair most blacks felt.

Some continued their search for dignity and justice as part of the Black Consciousness Movement. With its themes of "Black Is Beautiful" and "I'm Black and I'm Proud," the Black Consciousness Movement inspired new calls for black nationalism and black separatism.

"The Second Reconstruction" Betrayed (1973-1992)

For the most part, the 1970s and 1980s cast a shadow over the dreams of black Americans for racial justice and equality. With the exception of Jimmy Carter's presidency from 1976 to 1980, it was a time when blacks first felt neglected, then threatened. There was little attempt to enforce existing civil rights laws, for example, and very few blacks were named to top positions in the federal government. (They did make progress in local politics, however, especially in the South.) Schools and businesses felt less pressure to recruit minorities to make up for the unfair practices of the past, especially after white men began to complain about "reverse discrimination." And Republican presidents from Richard Nixon through George Bush suggested that blacks' problems stemmed less from racism than from a need for more initiative, self-reliance, and economic development within the black community.

Jimmy Carter's election to the presidency in 1976 held out the promise of a new way of thinking. While he did name several blacks to high-level positions, President Carter came under fire for not doing enough to help the vast majority of African Americans. A shaky economy marked by high inflation and gasoline shortages hit blacks especially hard during his administration. The Iran hostage crisis of 1979 added to the nation's depressed mood and paved the way for a return to Republican control of the White House in 1980.

Under the new president, Ronald Reagan, blacks once again found themselves shut out of the highest levels of government. Although he insisted that his moves to strengthen the economy helped all Americans, black as well as white, President Reagan opposed or ignored many issues of interest to black Americans. He appointed conservative judges to various federal courts (including the Supreme Court) who struck down many programs that had been designed to make up for past discrimination against minorities.

At first, black Americans who felt abandoned by their government turned instead to the major civil rights organizations for leadership. But the marches and court decisions that had been so effective during the 1950s and 1960s did not have the same impact during the 1970s and 1980s, and the riots had not led to any major improvements. Many blacks seemed resigned to the fact that America was still a nation of two societies—one black, one white—separate and unequal. The increase in racially motivated violence against blacks during the 1980s supported this belief that racism was alive and well in America.

Discouraged by these setbacks, some blacks decided that the only way to make progress on issues of importance to African Americans was to reject traditional politics. A few looked into alternative movements, including the Nation of Islam and Afrocentrism, which stressed the value of black culture and the black experience (especially its African roots).

One who chose a different path was Jesse Jackson, a minister and veteran civil rights activist who had become the most popular national black leader since Martin Luther King, Jr. In 1984, he campaigned for the Democratic nomination for president of the United States. Even though he lost in a bitter fight to former vice-president Walter Mondale (who later lost the presidential election to Ronald Reagan), Jackson inspired thousands of blacks at a time when they had just about given up on politics. And his candidacy proved that it was possible for an African American to seek the nomination of a major party.

By the late 1980s, blacks were mayors of almost all of the country's larger cities and some of its smaller ones, too. Black representation in state legislatures, school boards, and state courts was also increasing, especially in the South. Encouraged by these trends, Jesse Jackson decided to run again for the Democratic presidential nomination in 1988.

This time, Jackson made a special effort to reach out to the people who had not supported him in 1984. He was much more successful in the primaries and ended up finishing a strong second in the delegate count. This gave him enough power to help shape the Democratic platform, or its statement of policies and principles. He was also able to make sure that blacks received some high-ranking jobs in the party. Most of all, his success continued to reduce the feeling among many African Americans that they had been shut out of politics at the national level. But at election time, the Republicans once again captured the White House.

After George Bush took office as president in January, 1989, some blacks thought he would reverse the trends of the Reagan years and revive the "Second Reconstruction." The early signs were hopeful. He named General Colin Powell head of the Joint Chiefs of Staff and made Dr. Louis Sullivan secretary of Health and Human Services. He repeatedly expressed his admiration for the ideals of Martin Luther King, Jr., and observed the national holiday honoring the slain civil rights activist. And in 1990, he welcomed African National Congress leader Nelson Mandela to the White House.

But by mid-1990, many blacks had begun to question President Bush's sincerity on issues of importance to African Americans. For example, they thought he was too eager to support the white minority government in South Africa. They were outraged when he vetoed the 1991 Civil Rights Bill because it contained what he felt were unconstitutional employment quotas. In addition, many blacks did not support America's involvement in the Persian Gulf War or the nomination of Clarence Thomas to the U.S. Supreme Court.

Years of anger and frustration came to a head in April, 1992, after four white Los Angeles policemen were found not guilty in the 1991 beating of black motorist Rodney King. Los Angeles experienced the worst riot in American history. Disturbances broke out in several other cities, too. Not since the civil rights era of the 1950s and 1960s had there been so much protest. And for a short time at least, the dismal conditions faced by urban blacks received national attention.

Toward a Black Agenda (1993 and Beyond)

By the time of the 1992 presidential election, the ongoing economic recession, not the Los Angeles riot, was the topic on everyone's mind. That November, a large number of white voters joined with an overwhelming majority of black voters to demand change. They turned Republican George Bush out of office after only one term and elected Democrat Bill Clinton instead. Also as a result of the elections, the Congressional Black Caucus grew from twenty-five members to thirty-nine. For the first time, the group appeared to be in a position to exercise a considerable amount of power, especially with a Democrat in the White House.

Although President Clinton chose several blacks and other minorities for positions in his cabinet, many African Americans adopted a "wait-and-see" attitude toward the new administration. Some questioned the sincerity of Clinton's commitment to a "Black Agenda." They pointed out that he campaigned heavily among middle-class whites, avoided Jesse Jackson and other more outspoken black leaders, and never presented any concrete plans for dealing with problems unique to the black community.

In fact, President Clinton stumbled badly on a number of issues of importance to African Americans. Many blacks were upset by his decision to return Haitian refugees to their country— a policy he had condemned during the campaign. Others were disappointed by the defeat of his job creation bill, which they blamed on an ineffective White House strategy. Battles over the proposed budget for social programs also alienated many black leaders as the president ignored African American politicians and instead looked for support among moderate and conservative white Democrats.

Perhaps the biggest blow, however, came when President Clinton withdrew Lani Guinier's nomination to head the civil rights division of the Justice Department. Within days, angry members of the Congressional Black Caucus responded by announcing that the group was planning to "reassess" its relationship with the White House. As everyone continues to watch the direction President Clinton takes, black Americans in particular can be counted on to take up their concerns with both Congress and the new administration.

—Alton Hornsby, Jr. and Deborah Gillan Straub, August 1993

PHOTO CREDITS

The photographs and illustrations appearing in *African American Chronology* were received from the following sources:

On the covers: **UPI/Bettmann Newsphotos.**

Archive Photos: page 35; **Schomberg Center for Research in Black Culture, The New York Public Library, Astor, Lenox and Tilden Foundations:** pages 49, 50, 000; **National Archives:** pages 51, 99; **The Granger Collection, New York:** page 54; **AP/Wide World Photos:** pages 62, 70, 74, 82, 93, 106, 107, 110, 112, 117, 119, 125, 128, 135, 136, 138, 141, 189, 190, 219, 220, 236, 252, 258, 261, 266, 271, 304, 306, 313, 316, 321, 330, 333, 356; **The Bettmann Archive:** pages 63, 72; **UPI/Bettmann Newsphotos:** pages 68, 95, 114, 131, 133, 140, 142, 146, 147, 171, 205; **Bethune Museum and Archive:** page 77; **Photograph by Merrill A. Roberts, Jr:** page 81; **Photograph by Cecil Layne:** page 85; **Hurok Attractions:** page 86; **U.S. Air Force:** page 88; **U.S. Navy:** page 90; **New York Times Pictures:** page 103; **Bill Sparrow/*Encore* Magazine:** page 105; **Photograph by Carl Nesfeld:** page 126; **United Nations:** page 129; **Ace Creative Photos:** page 134; *Downbeat* **magazine:** page 143; **Photograph by Chester Higgins, Jr:** page 166; *New York Amsterdam News:* page 000; **Keystone Photos:** page 203; **William Morris Agency:** page 305; **(c) Scott Cunningham 1987:** page 307.

AFRICAN AMERICAN CHRONOLOGY

1492   Pedro Alonzo Niño, whom some historians think was black, arrived in the New World with explorer Christopher Columbus. Other blacks later sailed with Vasco Núñez de Balboa, Juan Ponce de Leon, Hernán Cortes, Francisco Pizarro, and Pedro Menéndez de Avilés on their travels to the Americas.

1502   Portugal delivered its first shipment of black slaves to the New World.

1526   The first group of blacks to set foot on what is now the United States arrived in present day South Carolina. They had been brought by a Spanish explorer to help build a settlement. But they soon escaped and went to live among the Native North Americans.

1538   Black explorer Estevanico (also known as Esteban) discovered what is now Arizona and New Mexico.

Estevanico was born in Morocco, a country in North Africa. As a slave, he was part of an expedition that left Spain in 1527 to explore the western coast of the Gulf of Mexico. But the explorers' ships were blown off course into what is now Tampa Bay, Florida.

Sailing west, they then became shipwrecked on Galveston Island off the Texas coast. Only four survivors, including Estevanico, were able to keep going. He was an especially valuable member of the group because he got

Slaves arrive in America

along well with the Indians they met along the way. The explorers finally reached Mexico City around 1536. There they thrilled Spanish officials with tales they had heard from the Indians about seven golden cities to the northwest, in a place called Cibola.

In 1539, explorer Francisco Coronado set out to find Cibola and conquer it. Estevanico guided the advance party. Sent out alone ahead of the others, he was the first to see what would one day be Arizona and New Mexico. But he died at the hands of the Zuñi Indians of Cibola, and the rest of the advance party went back to Mexico.

1562   Great Britain entered the slave trade when an Englishman named John Hawkins sold a large shipment of blacks to Spanish planters in Hispaniola, the island that is now home to the nations of Haiti and the Dominican Republic.

1619   **August 20.** A Dutch ship with twenty blacks aboard arrived at Jamestown, Virginia. They had been captured in Africa and sold as indentured servants. (Many poor whites suffered the same fate.) Unlike slaves, who were considered the property of their owners, indentured servants usually worked for someone for seven years. At the end of that time, they gained their freedom.

The blacks who were brought to Jamestown against their will were the first permanent settlers of their race in what would one day become the United States. The history of African Americans begins with their arrival.

Advertisement for a slave auction

1641   Massachusetts became the first colony in North America to recognize slavery as a legal institution.

1661   Virginia recognized slavery as a legal institution and established strict "slave codes," or laws. These codes left blacks with almost no rights. Generally, they could not leave the plantation or gather in groups without permission. They could not own weapons and could not testify against white people in court. Slaves found guilty of murder or rape were executed. For less serious crimes, they were whipped, mutilated, or branded.

1663   **September 13.** A servant in Gloucester County, Virginia, revealed that a group of white servants and black slaves had been plotting to overthrow their master. It was the first recorded conspiracy of its kind in colonial America.

1704   Elias Nau, a Frenchman living in New York City, established one of the first schools in the colonies that was open to slaves.

1712   **April 7.** A black slave revolt occurred in New York City.

It began when a group of armed slaves met in an orchard near the center of the city and set fire to an outhouse owned by a white man. The blacks then shot and killed some whites who tried to put out the fire. Twenty-one of the twenty-seven slaves involved were captured and executed. The other six committed suicide.

1731   Benjamin Banneker, a noted mathematician, astronomer, inventor, and writer, was born in Ellicott, Maryland.

The grandson of a white woman, Banneker received his basic education at a school for free blacks near Joppa, Maryland. He then taught himself other mechanical and scientific principles by taking apart and building various objects. Years later, when he was well into his fifties, he borrowed some astronomical instruments from a neighbor and learned calculus and trigonometry.

Building on this new knowledge, Banneker wrote and published a popular astronomical almanac every year between 1791 and 1802. His other writings include a report on bees as well as the first material on astronomy published by a black man in the United States. He is also credited with figuring out the cycle of the seventeen-year locust.

In 1791, on the recommendation of Thomas Jefferson, Banneker became a member of the commission that developed plans for the layout of Washington, D.C. Later that same year, he wrote a famous letter to Jefferson in which he appealed for a change in whites' attitudes toward blacks. Pointing to his own work as proof, Banneker declared that blacks were not mentally inferior to whites. At first, Jefferson seemed to accept the possibility. Later, he rejected the idea and even expressed doubts about Banneker's intelligence.

Banneker died in 1806.

1739   **September 9.** The first serious slave uprising in the colonies took place near Charleston, South Carolina.

Led by a black man named Cato, it began when some slaves killed two warehouse guards, stole guns and ammunition, and marched toward Florida. They killed all whites who tried to stop them along the way. All but about a dozen of the slaves were eventually captured. More than thirty others were killed because they were thought to be involved in the revolt.

1761   **December 15.** Jupiter Hammon published the first known work of poetry by an American black, *Salvation by Christ with Penitential Cries*. Hammon had been born a slave in 1720.

1770   **March 5.** Escaped slave Crispus Attucks died along with four other Americans in the Boston Massacre.

Attucks was at the head of a group of angry colonists who were taunting British soldiers. One of the soldiers then panicked and fired his gun. Attucks and two other men fell to the ground, fatally wounded. (The remaining two men died later of their injuries.) The state of Massachusetts later honored Attucks with a statue in Boston.

1773   Former slaves George Leile and Andrew Bryan organized the first Negro Baptist Church in the American colonies at Savannah, Georgia.

Phillis Wheatley, an African-born poet, became the first American black woman (and only the second American woman of any race) to publish a book. Its title was *Poems on Various Subjects, Religious and Moral*.

Born in Senegal around 1753, she was sold as a slave in 1761 to a Boston, Massachusetts tailor named John Wheatley. His wife taught the frail young girl to

4

The death of Crispus Attucks at the Boston Massacre

read and write and was surprised at how quickly she mastered those skills and how eager she was to learn more. The Wheatleys then gave up their idea of making Phillis a servant and instead encouraged her to study the Bible as well as classical and contemporary literature.

By the time she reached her early teens, Phillis was writing her own poetry. Her first poem was published in Boston in 1770. It brought her national and then international attention after it was reprinted in newspapers throughout the American colonies as well as in England.

In 1773, Wheatley visited London, England, where she was treated like a celebrity and taken to meet the lord mayor and other important people. One of them, an English abolitionist named Selina Hastings, arranged for the publication of *Poems on Various Subjects, Religious and Moral.*

Wheatley was freed just a few months before her mistress died in March, 1774. She continued to write poems, mostly in honor of famous people and events. After writing one about George Washington, for example, she was invited to meet with him on February 28, 1776, so that he could thank her in person. But even though Washington and others praised her work, Wheatley could not find anyone who would publish her poetry.

In 1778, Wheatley married a free black man named John Peters. When he experienced financial problems and was thrown into debtor's prison, his wife struggled to make a living for herself and their three small children as a house servant. Never a very strong or healthy person, Wheatley died on December 5, 1784. Two of her children had died before she did, and the third died shortly afterward and was buried with her.

Phillis Wheatley

1775 **April 14.** The first abolitionist society in the United States was organized in Philadelphia, Pennsylvania. ("Abolitionist" comes from the word "abolish," or get rid of completely.) Known as the Pennsylvania Society for the Abolition of Slavery, it tried to prevent free blacks from being kidnapped and sold into slavery. It was also successful in getting antislavery laws passed in the state of Pennsylvania.

April 19. The American War for Independence began in Massachusetts near the villages of Lexington and Concord. Blacks were among the first colonial soldiers (known as Minutemen) who fought against the British.

May. Members of the Continental Congress (a group of men who represented each of the colonies in a type of national government) declared that only free blacks could serve in the Revolutionary Army.

June 17. Two blacks, Peter Salem and Salem Poor, were officially recognized as heroes for their efforts on behalf of the colonists at the Battle of Bunker Hill. Peter Salem's contribution was especially important, because he was the man who killed the British commander, Major John Pitcairn. While Pitcairn's death did not help the Americans win the battle, it did raise their spirits and inspire them to keep fighting.

July 9. General George Washington announced that blacks would no longer be allowed to enlist in the Revolutionary Army.

October 23. The Continental Congress approved General George Washington's decision to exclude blacks from the Revolutionary Army.

November 7. Lord Dunmore, the British royal governor of Virginia, promised freedom to all slaves who joined the British forces in the Revolutionary War. Southerners, especially Virginians, were frightened and angry. They urged blacks

Peter Salem shoots Major Pitcairn at the Battle of Bunker Hill

to ignore the offer and remain loyal to the colonies.

Historians are not sure how many slaves actually took the British up on their offer, but they do know that at least 100,000 blacks ran away from their masters during the war.

December 31. General George Washington changed his mind and decided to allow free blacks to join the Revolutionary Army. More than 5,000 blacks eventually served. Most of them were from the northern colonies.

1776   **July 4.** In Philadelphia, Pennsylvania, the Continental Congress approved the Declaration of Independence.

1777   **July 2.** Vermont became the first state to abolish slavery. By 1804, all of the states north of Delaware had taken steps to abolish slavery gradually. (As late as 1860, however, there were still some slaves in New Jersey.)

1787   **April 12.** Richard Allen and Absalom Jones founded the Free African Society. This black self-help group was probably the first stable, independent organization of its kind in the United States.

Richard Allen was perhaps the most famous black leader in the country before the rise of Frederick Douglass during the mid-1800s. Besides helping to establish the Free African Society, he was a co-founder of the African Methodist Episcopal (AME) Church. (Also see entries dated June 10, 1794, and April 9, 1816.) He and Absalom Jones, a former slave who had bought his freedom, were close associates for many years.

One Sunday in 1786, the two men were attending services at a Philadelphia Methodist church when they and other worshippers were ordered to move to the blacks-only section in the balcony. Their response to this rejection was to form the Free African Society.

The Free African Society was a partly religious, partly social group that offered blacks help with burial expenses, aid for widows and orphans, and opportunities to strengthen marriage and family ties. It also kept in touch with abolitionist societies and free blacks in other areas of the country. In 1793, for example, the Free African Society organized relief efforts for Philadelphia blacks during a yellow fever epidemic. And during the War of 1812, members assembled a company of black soldiers.

July 13. The Continental Congress banned slavery in the Northwest Territory. This was the area between the Mississippi River, the Great Lakes, and the Ohio River.

September 12. Revolutionary War veteran Prince Hall received official approval from Freemasons in England to establish the first Masonic lodge for blacks. (The Free-

Richard Allen

masons are a group of men bound together by secret rituals who promise to help people in need.)

The son of an Englishman and a free black woman, Hall was born in Barbados, West Indies, in 1735. He was originally apprenticed as a leather worker but gave it up to move to Boston, Massachusetts.

During the Revolutionary War, a group of British soldiers admitted Hall and twelve other free blacks into a Masonic lodge. After the soldiers had to leave the area, Hall organized a new lodge for blacks. The group was chartered in England as African Lodge No. 459. Hall served as its first master and later set up other lodges in Pennsylvania and Rhode Island.

Hall did much to improve his community. For example, he was active in the movement to abolish slavery in Massachusetts and proposed laws to protect free blacks from kidnapping and enslavement. He also called for the establishment of schools for black children in Boston.

After Hall's death in 1807, the African Grand Lodge was renamed the Prince Hall Grand Lodge in his honor. It is still one of black America's major social institutions.

September. Representatives of the former colonies approved the Constitution of the United States.

Two sections in particular had an impact on African Americans. One of them discussed how the U.S. House of Representatives would be assembled. The constitution said that the number of representatives a state would have depended on the state's population. Each free person counted as one whole person, but slaves were counted as just three-fifths of a person. Another section of the constitution allowed the slave trade to continue until 1808.

1790   Jean Baptiste Point DuSable bought property in what is now Chicago, Illinois. There he established a fur trading post, making him the area's first permanent settler.

A native of St. Marc, Haiti, DuSable was born in 1745. He was the son of a French businessman and a black slave. DuSable went to school in France and later worked for his father in New Orleans, Louisiana.

When the Spanish took over Louisiana from the French in 1765, DuSable and a friend headed north for other French-settled areas along the Mississippi River. They stopped at what is now St. Louis, Missouri, where they carried on a successful fur trade with the Indians for two years before moving farther north.

Jean Baptiste Point DuSable and his fur trading settlement

In 1772, DuSable decided to build a fur trading post on the Chicago River near Lake Michigan. It soon became a very busy trading center, and eventually the settlement of Chicago sprang up around the post. After the Illinois territory came under the control of the United States, DuSable sold his property and returned to Missouri. He died there in 1818.

1793   **February 12.** The U.S. Congress passed the first Fugitive Slave Act. This law made it a crime to hide an escaped slave or to interfere with his or her arrest.

March 14. Eli Whitney, a white inventor from Massachusetts, obtained a patent for his cotton gin.

Whitney's machine separated cotton from the seeds, hull, and other material, a job that had been done by hand up to that time. It helped make the business of growing cotton much more profitable. As a result, planters expanded their farms and bought more and more slaves to work in the fields. This made the slave system even stronger, especially in the South.

1794   **June 10.** Richard Allen of Philadelphia founded the Bethel African Methodist Episcopal Church, the first AME church in the United States. (Also see entries dated April 12, 1787, and April 9, 1816.)

1797   **January 30.** Blacks from North Carolina presented a petition to the U.S. Congress protesting a state law that required freed slaves to be returned to North Carolina and to the status of slavery. This was the first recorded antislavery petition by blacks. Congress rejected it.

1800   **August 30.** Near Richmond, Virginia, bad weather and betrayal forced Gabriel Prosser and Jack Bowler to call off their plans for a slave uprising.

As many as 1,000 blacks had been ready to take part in what would have been one of the biggest slave revolts in American history. Prosser had hoped to capture an arsenal (a building where weapons and military equipment are manufactured or stored) at Richmond, kill whites in the area, and free the slaves. They were almost ready to launch their attack when a severe rainstorm hit the area and made it hard for many of them to make it to the place where they were all supposed to meet. In addition, two slaves who had begun to have second thoughts about killing their master betrayed Prosser and the others. So the governor of Virginia called out the state militia to track down the plotters.

Most of them—including Prosser—were eventually captured, convicted, and sentenced to hang. Even though he was questioned by the governor himself, Prosser refused to name any of the other slaves who had conspired with him. He was executed on October 7, 1800.

1804   The Ohio legislature passed the first "Black Laws." These were intended to restrict the rights of free blacks in the North.

Many northern blacks had enjoyed a fair amount of freedom since the days of the Revolutionary War and the Declaration of Independence. But the liberal attitudes toward them faded as the years passed. By 1835, several northern states had made it difficult or impossible for free blacks to vote or move from one place to another. By 1860, they faced so many restrictions that they were hardly better off than slaves.

1808   **January 1.** A federal law went into effect that banned traders from importing African slaves into the United States. Punishment for breaking the new law included fines or prison terms. But the government did not try very hard to enforce it, and slave traders continued their business without much interference.

1812   Martin R. Delany, pioneer black physician, colonizationist, and Union Army officer, was born in Virginia.

Delany received his medical degree from Harvard University in 1852. He then moved to Pittsburgh, Pennsylvania, and tried to set up a medical practice. But prejudice made it difficult for him to earn a living, and he eventually had to leave town.

Delany then became a member of the British Association for the Promotion of Social Science. He also published two books, including *The Condition, Elevation, Emigration and Destiny of the Colored People of the United States*. A leader in the national convention movement of black Americans (see entry dated September 20-24, 1830), Delany worked with abolitionist Frederick Douglass on the *North Star* newspaper.

After the U.S. Congress passed the Compromise of 1850 and its tougher fugitive slave law (see entry dated September 18, 1850), Delany decided that the United States was becoming more and more unfriendly and dangerous for people of African descent. So he turned his efforts toward colonization instead. He helped organize an expedition to Nigeria in 1858 and talked eight African chiefs into giving some land to prospective black settlers from America. He also made plans to grow more cotton in the area and export it.

During the American Civil War, Delany served as a medical officer with a Union Army regiment in South Carolina. He remained in the state after the war, settling in Charleston. There he worked for the Freedmen's Bureau and later served as a justice of the peace. In 1874, Delany lost in an attempt to become lieutenant governor of South Carolina. He died in 1885.

1816   **April 9.** The African Methodist Episcopal (AME) Church, the first all-black religious denomination in the United States, formally organized in Philadelphia, Pennsylvania. Richard Allen was named its first bishop.

Born a slave in Philadelphia, Allen was sold as a youth to a white man from Delaware. He became a preacher not long after that and received permission to hold services in his master's home. There he preached to both blacks and whites. He also hired himself out to other congregations. Allen eventually bought his freedom by hauling salt, wood, and other products and by working in a brickyard. With Absalom Jones, he founded the Free African Society in 1787.

Allen served as head of the AME Church for fifteen years, until his death in 1831. (Also see entries dated April 12, 1787; June 10, 1794; and September 20-24, 1830.)

December 28. The American Colonization Society was organized in Washington, D.C. Among its sponsors were two well-known members of the U.S. House of Representatives—John Calhoun of South Carolina and Henry Clay of Kentucky.

The group's goal was to ease American racial problems by sending free blacks to settle in Africa. Many blacks strongly protested this attempt to make them leave their native country.

1817   Black shipbuilder, civil rights activist, and African colonizer Paul Cuffe died.

Cuffe had been born a free man in New Bedford, Massachusetts, in 1758. His father had been a slave who was born in Africa, and his mother was a Native North American.

Early on in life, Cuffe decided that the business world offered greater possibilities for wealth and influence than farming did. So he trained himself in navigation and mathematics and eventually earned his fortune as a whaler and trader in the Americas and Europe. He also became an activist on behalf of his people. Together with his brother, for example, Cuffe sued the state of Massachusetts for the right to vote. And in 1797, he bought a farm and built a school for the children in his hometown of Westport, Massachusetts. Much of what he tried to do was shaped by his Quaker faith. The Quakers (also known as the Society of Friends) are a religious group known for their devotion to peace and helping others. They were among the first people in the colonies to call for the abolition of slavery.

Although he received a great deal of support from the Quakers in his efforts to end discrimination, Cuffe grew more and more discouraged about the future of free blacks in America. Eventually, he began to look toward Africa in the belief that colonization was the answer. In 1811, he took a group of thirty-eight blacks to Sierra Leone, a British colony on the west coast of Africa. But failing health and doubts about whether his plan could really succeed led him to back out of the venture not long before his death.

Cuffe left an estate valued at more than $20,000. This made him one of the richest blacks in early American history.

1820   **March 3.** The U.S. Congress approved the famous Missouri Compromise. It outlawed slavery within the Louisiana Purchase territory north of 36° 30' latitude (see map on next page). Missouri itself entered the Union as a slave state, while Maine entered as a free state.

1821   With the support of the American Colonization Society, the black Republic of Liberia was established in West Africa. American blacks were encouraged to move there to help lessen racial tensions in the United States. But only about 20,000 people ended up going.

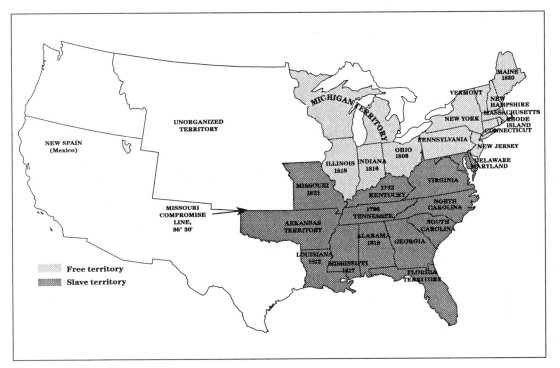

The United States and neighboring territories around 1820

1822   **May 30.** A slave conspiracy led by Denmark Vesey in Charleston, South Carolina, fell apart after someone alerted the authorities.

Vesey, a former slave, had been free since 1800. He worked as a sailor and carpenter in Charleston. He plotted his slave uprising for several years, collecting weapons and carefully choosing who to let in on the plan until as many as 5,000 blacks were involved.

Vesey and thirty-six other participants were hanged for their roles in the conspiracy. And to make it even harder for any future plotters, South Carolina and several other states tightened the controls on free blacks and slaves.

1827   **March 16.** In New York City, John Russwurm (the first black to graduate from an American college) and Samuel Cornish began publishing the nation's first black newspaper, *Freedom's Journal*. Like most of the black publications founded before the Civil War, *Freedom's Journal* was primarily an antislavery propaganda sheet.

It was not very successful, and within a couple of years Cornish had turned his attention to other projects.

1829

Copies of *An Appeal to the Colored People of the World,* David Walker's militant antislavery pamphlet calling on blacks to revolt, appeared in several southern states and caused an uproar among slave owners.

Walker was a free black who had wandered across the South before settling in Boston, Massachusetts. There he owned a used-clothing store and studied antislavery and revolutionary literature.

In *An Appeal to the Colored People of the World,* he urged slaves to rise up and take violent revenge against slave owners. Black sailors were probably responsible for smuggling copies of it into the South. Even though few blacks knew how to read, fearful authorities took no chances. They watched the mails, searched all ships docking at southern ports, and restricted black sailors. Circulating *An Appeal to the Colored People of the World* became a crime, and a bounty was placed on Walker's life. He died under mysterious circumstances in 1830.

1830

April 6. James Augustine Healy, the first black Catholic bishop in America, was born on a plantation near Macon, Georgia.

Healy was the son of an Irish immigrant and a woman of mixed black and white heritage. His father sent him and his brothers up north for their education to a Quaker school on New York's Long Island. Later, they attended the College of the Holy Cross in Worcester, Massachusetts, where young James was the best student. In 1852, he entered the Sulpician Seminary in Paris, France. It was in the French capital, at Notre Dame Cathedral, that Healy was ordained a priest on June 10, 1854.

Returning to Massachusetts, Healy went to work as a priest in a white parish in Boston, then became secretary to the Bishop of Boston. When the bishop died, Healy took over as pastor of the New St. James Church.

Energetic and devoted to duty, Healy continued to rise up through the ranks of the Catholic Church, becoming bishop of Maine in 1875. Although he ministered to an all-white following, he experienced only occasional problems with racial prejudice. Shortly before his death on August 5, 1890, Healy was promoted to the rank of assistant at the papal throne.

September 20-24. The first National Negro Convention met at Bethel AME

Church in Philadelphia, Pennsylvania. Delegates from Delaware, Maryland, New York, Pennsylvania, and Virginia attended. Under the leadership of Richard Allen (see entry dated April 9, 1816), the group adopted resolutions calling for improvements in the social status of American blacks.

Despite the fact that some blacks questioned the need for them, the conventions continued over the years. Sometimes, white abolitionists and reformers also attended. In the decade before the Civil War, for example, many such meetings were held across the North. (Also see entry dated July 6-8, 1853.)

1831   **January 1.** White abolitionist William Lloyd Garrison published the first issue of the *Liberator,* a militant antislavery newspaper. He received financial aid and moral support from a number of prominent blacks, including James Forten of Philadelphia, Pennsylvania.

August 21-22. Black minister Nat Turner, a slave who had once run away from his master but then decided to return, led the most famous slave revolt in American history. The uprising in Southampton County, Virginia, resulted in the deaths of about sixty whites. Turner was captured on October 30 and hanged on November 11. Thirty other blacks who conspired with him were also executed.

The aftermath left the South near chaos. Authorities vigorously enforced slave codes. Slave patrols increased, and suspicious blacks were either jailed or killed. As a result, there were no other major slave revolts until John Brown's raid on the U.S. arsenal at Harpers Ferry, Virginia, in 1859.

1838   **March 14.** Blacks held a mass meeting in Philadelphia to protest the action of the Pennsylvania Reform Convention of 1837 that denied them the right to vote.

The action was based on a State Supreme Court decision that said blacks were not freemen and that only white males could vote. Despite the outcry, the court decision was not overturned, and the state of Pennsylvania adopted a new constitution that denied blacks the vote.

Frank Johnson, one of America's first black bandleaders, gave a command performance before England's Queen Victoria at Buckingham Palace.

Born in 1792, Johnson established himself as a versatile musician playing with

Nat Turner's capture

white bands in Philadelphia, Pennsylvania. When he organized his own group, known as Frank Johnson's Colored Band, it earned national acclaim for its performances at parades and dances. The band even played at plantations as far south as Virginia. In addition to being a musician, Johnson was also a composer. He died in 1844.

1839   **July.** The most famous slave mutiny in American history took place on the Spanish ship *Amistad*. It involved a group of fifty-three Africans who had been bought by two Spaniards in violation of international laws against slave trading.

The incident began when the slaves—led by a man named Joseph Cinque—took over the *Amistad* after it left Cuba and ordered the crew to sail it back to Africa. Instead, the crew tricked the slaves by changing course at night. Eventually, the *Amistad* ended up near Montauk, Long Island, New York, where it was intercepted by an American ship. The rebels were arrested and imprisoned while government officials tried to decide what to do about them. Some wanted to send them back to Cuba to be put on trial. But abolitionists and their supporters favored giving them a trial in America.

The case went all the way to the U.S. Supreme Court. There, former president John Quincy Adams argued that the Africans should be granted their freedom. The Court agreed, saying that since they had been illegally enslaved and had tried to escape, they deserved to be considered free under American law.

Joseph Cinque

1843   **August 22.** At a national convention of black men in Buffalo, New York, black abolitionist minister Henry Highland Garnet called for a slave revolt and a general strike to improve conditions for blacks across the United States. Many of the delegates, including Frederick Douglass, condemned the speech.

1846   **August.** Black inventor Norbert Rillieux obtained his first patent on a revolutionary process that made it possible to refine sugar whiter and grainier. The technique became standard in the sugar industry as well as in other industries.

Born in New Orleans, Louisiana, in 1806, Rillieux was the son of a white engineer and inventor and a free woman of mixed black and white heritage. He went to school in Paris, France, and in 1810 he began teaching applied mathematics at the L'Ecole Centrale there. He probably developed the theory behind his future invention about this time.

Later, Rillieux returned to the United States and began testing his process on a Louisiana plantation in 1834. He finalized his invention in 1845 and patented it the next year.

Frustrated by the racial discrimination he experienced in Louisiana, Rillieux went back to Paris in 1861. He died in France in 1894.

1847   **June 30.** In St. Louis, Missouri, Dred Scott filed a lawsuit claiming that because he had lived for a while in a free territory, he deserved to be considered a free man.

Scott was a semi-literate slave who had roamed throughout the country. He based his suit on the fact that his travels had taken him through free Illinois as well as free portions of the Louisiana territory. (Also see entry dated March 6, 1857.)

Dred Scott

December 3. Leading black abolitionist Frederick Douglass began publishing his own newspaper, the *North Star*.

Born in Tuckahoe, Maryland, in 1817, Douglass was separated from his mother while he was still a baby and raised by harsh masters. As a youngster, he worked as a house servant in Baltimore, Maryland, and learned to read from his white playmates. His first attempt to escape failed, but a second try in 1838 was successful.

Frederick Douglass

Douglass continued his education among antislavery groups in the North and eventually became a skilled speaker and writer. The launching of the *North Star* was one of the reasons behind Douglass's break with William Lloyd Garrison, a white abolitionist and publisher of an antislavery newspaper called the *Liberator*. Garrison opposed the *North Star* because he did not see the need for a second major antislavery publication. But Douglass and other blacks felt that establishing their own newspaper was a way for them to play a more important role in the abolitionist movement.

In his later years, Douglass served in several political and diplomatic posts, including unofficial advisor to presidents Abraham Lincoln and Andrew Johnson, marshal of the District of Columbia, recorder of deeds of the District of Columbia, and minister to Haiti. He also served as president of the Freedmen's Bank in 1874. (Also see entry dated February 20, 1895.)

1848   **February.** The United States and Mexico signed a peace treaty that ended two years of war.

Under the terms of the treaty, Mexico gave up the present states of Arizona, California, Nevada, New Mexico, Utah and parts of Colorado and Wyoming. This touched off an immediate and bitter debate between the North and the South over the issue of slavery in the new territories. The number of free states and slave states stood at fifteen each, so maintaining that shaky balance was crucial.

The controversy raged for the next two years and paved the way for the infamous Compromise of 1850. (Also see entry dated September 18, 1850.)

1849   **July.** Harriet Tubman escaped from slavery in Maryland.

The best-known black female abolitionist, Tubman was born in Dorchester County, Maryland, in 1823. While working as a field hand as a young girl, she received a severe head injury from a weight that an angry overseer had thrown at another slave. The damage from that blow caused her to suffer from "sleeping seizures" for the rest of her life.

In 1844, she married a free black man named John Tubman but remained a slave herself. After her master died in 1849 and rumors spread that his slaves were going to be sold to someone in the Deep South, Tubman and two of her brothers escaped. Afraid of punishment, her brothers soon returned to the plantation. But Tubman marched on until she reached Philadelphia, Pennsylvania.

In 1850, Tubman went back to Maryland for a sister and a brother. The next year, she led eleven blacks to freedom in Canada. (By this time, her husband had married another woman, so she left him behind.) In 1857, Tubman made one of her last trips to Maryland, rescuing her parents and three more brothers and sisters. All told, Tubman made at least twenty trips into Maryland and Virginia and is credited with freeing more than 300 slaves through the so-called "Underground Railroad." (The Underground Railroad didn't really involve trains or anything underground. The term referred to a secret network of safe places such as houses or barns where runaway slaves could hide on their way north. These safe places were called "stations," and people like Tubman were the "conductors.")

After serving in the Civil War as a nurse and a spy, Tubman finally rejoined her family at their new home in Auburn, New York. She devoted the rest of her life to turning her house into a shelter for elderly and poor blacks. (Also see entry dated March 10, 1913.)

Benjamin Roberts, a black parent in Boston, Massachusetts, sued the city for not allowing his daughter to attend a white public school. The State Supreme Court rejected his suit and established the "separate-but-equal" doctrine instead. (Also see entry dated May 18, 1896.)

Peter Lowery became pastor of a black church in Nashville, Tennessee, making him probably the first black pastor of a church in the South. Born a slave, he had bought his freedom and that of other members of his family over a period of more than forty years.

Harriet Tubman (at far left) with some slaves she helped to escape

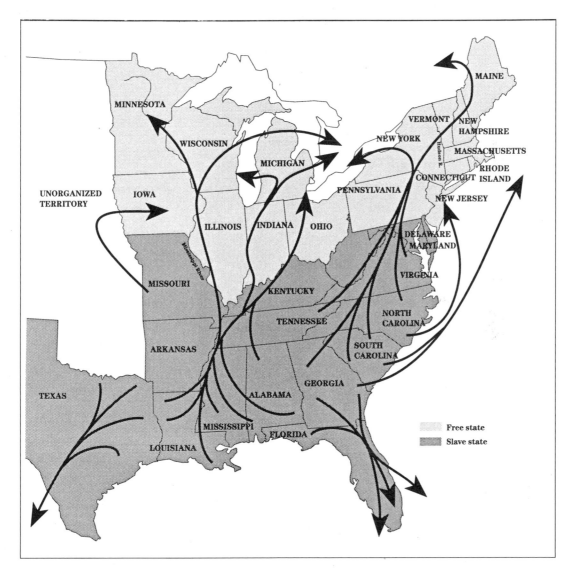

Underground Railroad routes

1850   **September 18.** The U.S. Congress enacted the famous Compromise of 1850.

Senator Henry Clay of Kentucky and other "moderate" statesmen from both North and South had come up with the Compromise as a solution to the problem of slavery in the new territories of New Mexico and California. It outlawed the slave trade in Washington, D.C., but kept it everywhere else throughout the South. In addition, California was admitted to the Union as a free state, and a new and tougher fugitive slave law replaced the poorly enforced Fugitive Slave Act of 1793. (Also see entries dated February 12, 1793, and February 7, 1848.)

Tracking down a runaway slave

1851   Soprano Elizabeth Taylor Greenfield made her debut at a concert sponsored by the Buffalo (New York) Musical Association.

The most famous black concert artist of her time, Greenfield was born a slave in Natchez, Mississippi, in 1809. As a baby, she was taken to Philadelphia, Pennsylvania, and adopted by a Quaker woman named Greenfield who arranged for her to study music and sing at private parties.

After her Buffalo debut, Greenfield—known as the "Black Swan"—toured the northern states between 1851 and 1853. In 1854, she went to England and gave a command performance before Queen Victoria in Buckingham Palace.

1852   **March 20.** *Uncle Tom's Cabin,* a novel by a northern white woman named Harriet Beecher Stowe, was published in Boston, Massachusetts. With its dramatic exaggeration of the cruelties of slavery, it created sympathy for blacks in the North and greatly angered southerners.

1853   **July 6-8.** The National Council of Colored People was founded in Rochester, New York, as an offshoot of the Negro Convention Movement. While the conventions met only occasionally, the National Council of Colored People was a permanent organization devoted to advancing the cause of blacks.

At the Council's founding meeting, members issued a famous statement condemning racial oppression in America. They also pointed out examples of black progress and proposed setting up a national industrial training school for blacks. (Also see entry dated September 20-24, 1830.)

Former slave, abolitionist, historian, and physician William Wells Brown published *Clotel,* the first novel written by a black American. The story of a black woman whose father was an American president, the book is based on the legend that Thomas Jefferson fathered many children by his slave mistresses.

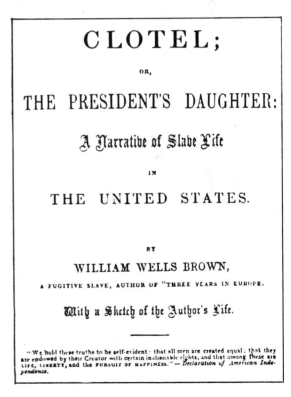

Title page from the first novel by an African American

Born in 1816 in Lexington, Kentucky, Brown himself was the son of a slave and a white slave owner. He went to school in St. Louis, Missouri, where he also worked for abolitionist editor Elijah P. Lovejoy. In addition to his novel, Brown published several other books, including *Three Years in Europe; or, Places I Have Seen and People I Have Met, The Black Man,* and *The Negro in the American Rebellions.* He also contributed regularly to newspapers such as the *Liberator,* the *London Daily News,* and the *National Anti-Slavery Standard.*

As an antislavery activist, Brown lectured and helped fleeing slaves to safety as a "conductor" on the Underground Railroad. He died in 1884.

1854　**January 1.** Lincoln University, the nation's first black college, was chartered as the Ashmum Institute in Oxford, Pennsylvania.

May 30. The U.S. Congress and President Franklin Pierce approved the Kansas-Nebraska Act.

Besides formally organizing the two territories of Kansas and Nebraska, the act repealed the Missouri Compromise of 1820. (See entry dated March 3, 1820.) Repealing the Compromise ended the ban on slavery north of 36°30' latitude in the Louisiana territory and paved the way for the people of territories like Kansas and Nebraska to decide for themselves whether to become free or slave states.

But people battled over the fate of Kansas for several years both in Congress and in the territory itself. (Some fights between pro- and antislavery forces even led to bloodshed.) On January 29, 1861, in a decision supported by a majority of its citizens, Kansas finally joined the Union as a free state.

1855　John Mercer Langston was elected clerk of Brownhelm Township in Lorain County, Ohio, making him the first black to be elected to a political office in the United States.

Langston was born to a white man and a black slave on a Virginia plantation in 1829. After his father died, young John was sent to Ohio, where he was raised by a family friend.

By 1854, Langston was practicing law in Chillicothe, Ohio, and in 1855, as the only black attorney in Brownhelm Township, he was elected clerk. He won a seat on the Brownhelm City Council the following year, a post he held until 1860. In 1865, he was named president of the National Equal Rights League, and in 1867 he became a member of the Board of Education in Oberlin, Ohio.

Langston returned to the South after the Civil War. He then held a variety of positions, including teacher, law school dean, and acting vice-president of Howard University from 1869 to 1876, minister to Haiti from 1877 to 1885, president of the Virginia Normal and Collegiate Institute from 1885 to 1888, and congressman from Virginia from 1889 to 1891. Langston died November 15, 1897. One of his most famous relatives was his grand-nephew, Harlem Renaissance poet Langston Hughes.

1857   **March 6.** The U.S. Supreme Court reached a decision in the case of *Dred Scott v. Sandford,* In a clear-cut victory for the South, the Court declared that blacks were not citizens of the United States. It also denied Congress the power to ban slavery in any federal territory.

The decision alarmed abolitionists in the North and helped increase the tensions that eventually led to the Civil War. As for Dred Scott, he remained a slave in St. Louis, Missouri, until he was freed by new owners. (Also see entry dated June 30, 1847.)

1859   **October 16.** Accompanied by a dozen white men and five blacks, white abolitionist John Brown attacked the U.S. Arsenal at Harpers Ferry, Virginia. (An arsenal is a building where weapons and military equipment are manufactured or stored.) His goal was to spark a widespread slave uprising.

Brown, a native of Kansas, had tried but failed to win the support of prominent abolitionists such as Frederick Douglass. Instead, local, state, and federal forces crushed the raid. Two blacks were killed for taking part in the attack,

John Brown on the way to his execution

and Brown himself was executed on December 2, 1859.

The *Clothilde,* the last slave ship to stop at an American port, landed at Mobile Bay, Alabama.

The U.S. Supreme Court, in *Ableman v. Booth,* overruled a decision by a Wisconsin state court declaring the Fugitive Slave Act of 1850 unconstitutional. (See entry dated September 18, 1850.)

The Wisconsin case involved a journalist who had been arrested for rounding up a mob to free a captured runaway slave. The state court ordered officials to release the journalist, then ruled that the federal law was unconstitutional.

This case showed how northerners were becoming more and more opposed to the Fugitive Slave Act and the ways in which it was enforced. In an attempt to get around the law, many northern cities and states passed Personal Liberty Laws. These laws banned local authorities from helping capture runaway slaves and declared that northern jails could not be used to house them.

1860   **November 6.** Voters elected Abraham Lincoln president of the United States. During his campaign, he had called for a ban on expanding slavery into the new territories of the country but stopped short of proposing an immediate end to it in the South. Nevertheless, southerners considered him to be an abolitionist.

December 17. South Carolina seceded, or broke away, from the Union, partly because of Lincoln's election as president. Mississippi, Florida, Alabama, Georgia, Louisiana, and Texas followed in January and February of 1861.

1861   **February 10.** Jefferson Davis was named president of the newly formed Confederate States of America, made up of the seven southern states that had left the Union since December, 1860.

April 12. In the first battle of the Civil War, the Confederates attacked Fort Sumter off the coast of Charleston, South Carolina, after they were unable to persuade the Union commander there to surrender. In little more than a day, the rebel bombs forced the sixty-eight-member Union force to give up and sail north.

President Abraham Lincoln immediately called for 75,000 volunteers to defend the Union. Many blacks saw the conflict as a war for freedom, and some rushed to join the Union forces. But they were turned down because of their race.

April 18. Virginia joined the Confederacy, followed by Tennessee, Arkansas, and North Carolina. This brought the total number of Confederate states to eleven. Twenty-three states remained in the Union.

August 23. James Stone, a very light-complexioned fugitive slave who was taken for a white man, enlisted in the First Fight Artillery of Ohio. He fought for the Union in Kentucky, where he had been a slave, and died from a service-related illness in 1862.

After his death, some blacks revealed Stone's true racial identity. Therefore, Stone was the first black man to fight for the North during the Civil War—almost two full years before blacks were officially allowed to join the Union Army.

September 25. The Secretary of the Navy approved the enlistment of blacks in the Navy.

1862

March 6. President Abraham Lincoln proposed to Congress a plan that would pay slave owners to free their slaves. He saw it as a slow process that would eventually eliminate slavery.

Representatives from the border states of Delaware, Kentucky, Maryland, Missouri, and West Virginia opposed the plan. Northern abolitionists did, too, because they felt slave owners should not be paid for property that they could not rightfully own. Nevertheless, the U.S. Congress passed a joint resolution on April 10, 1862, supporting the president's idea.

April 16. The U.S. Senate passed a bill abolishing slavery in the District of Columbia. The bill promised to pay slave owners $300 per slave. It also set aside $100,000 to help the newly freed men and women move to Haiti or Liberia if they wanted to leave the United States.

May 13. Robert Smalls, a black ship's pilot, sailed a Confederate steamer known as the *Planter* out of Charleston, South Carolina, and turned it over to the United States.

A former slave, Smalls was a member of a crew in the Confederate Navy when he performed his Civil War heroics. After the war, he was active in business and politics in South Carolina. He later served five terms in the U.S. House of Representatives.

June 19. President Abraham Lincoln signed a bill abolishing slavery in the federal territories.

July 17. The U.S. Congress authorized President Abraham Lincoln to accept blacks for service in the Union Army. But they agreed that blacks were to be paid less than white soldiers. A white soldier, for example, received $13 a month plus $3.50 for clothing, while blacks of the same rank received only $7 a month in pay plus $3 for clothing.

Eventually, more than 186,000 blacks served in the Union Army. Approximately 38,000 died, many due to overwork and poor medical care.

A rifle company of black Union Army troops

August 14. President Abraham Lincoln held the first discussion by an American president with a group of blacks. He urged them to emigrate to Africa or Latin America, a suggestion many of them denounced.

September 22. President Abraham Lincoln issued a preliminary Emancipation Proclamation. (Emancipation refers to the act of freeing a person from something.) His proclamation gave the states and territories then at war against the Union until January 1, 1863, to stop fighting or they would lose their slaves through emancipation.

1863   **January 1.** Hoping to turn the tide of war in favor of the North, President Abraham Lincoln signed the Emancipation Proclamation. It declared slaves free in all states and territories then at war against the United States. (Slaves in states loyal to the Union were not freed.)

May 1. The Confederate Congress passed a resolution calling black troops and their officers criminals. This meant that captured black soldiers and their officers could be executed or enslaved.

May 27. Two black regiments from Louisiana consisting of former slaves freed by the Emancipation Proclamation made six unsuccessful charges on the Confederate fortifications at Port Hudson, Louisiana.

July 9. Eight black regiments played a very important role in the siege of Port Hudson, Louisiana. Its capture, along with the capture of Vicksburg, Mississippi, allowed the Union to control the Mississippi River.

July 13-16. Four days of rioting occurred in New York City in protest against the Union's Draft Law. The disturbance left more than 1,000 people—mostly blacks—dead or wounded.

The riot erupted over a part of the Draft Law that allowed a man to pay $300 to another man willing to substitute for him in the draft. Since poor white laborers (many of whom were Irish and German immigrants) could not afford to pay substitutes, they were the ones who were drafted most often. (At the time, blacks were ineligible for the draft.) Angry and frustrated, the poor whites struck out at the people—especially blacks—they thought would be taking their jobs once they were drafted.

During this period of racial tension, similar disturbances occurred in Boston, Massachusetts, where twenty people were killed or wounded, and in Troy, New York, where a ship with black servants aboard had to be rerouted to avoid being attacked.

July 30. President Abraham Lincoln warned that he would strike back if the Confederates continued to execute or enslave captured black soldiers.

The 54th Massachusetts Negro Regiment served a year without pay rather than accept less pay than white soldiers. The struggles of this heroic group of African American soldiers — the first black unit in the army — were depicted in the 1989 movie Glory. It starred Denzel Washington (who won an Academy Award for his performance), Morgan Freeman, and Matthew Broderick.

The 54th Massachusetts Negro Regiment attacking Fort Wagner in July, 1863 (inset photo is of Civil War hero Nicholas Biddle)

1864   **April 12.** Confederate forces under General Nathan Bedford Forrest captured Fort Pillow, Tennessee, and then massacred the Union's black troops.

June 15. The U.S. Congress passed a bill giving black troops the same salaries and supplies as white troops.

June 19. A black sailor, Joachim Pease, won the Congressional Medal of Honor for his role in the famous naval battle between the U.S.S. *Kearsage* and the U.S.S. *Alabama* off the coast of France.

By order of a court martial, black Sergeant William Walker of the 3rd South Carolina Regiment was shot for leading a protest against discriminatory pay for black soldiers.

President Abraham Lincoln suggested that "very intelligent" blacks and those who had "fought gallantly in our ranks" might be given the right to vote. But even by the time of Lincoln's death, no one had taken any steps to give freed blacks the vote.

1865 The "Black Laws" of Illinois were repealed. These laws, like similar ones in other northern states, restricted the freedom of movement and limited the civil and political rights of free blacks. John Jones, one of the wealthiest blacks in America, led the fight for repeal.

Jones was born free in Green City, North Carolina, in 1816. A self-educated man, he became a tailor's apprentice. He worked first in Memphis, Tennessee, before moving to Chicago in 1845. There he opened a tailoring business and became very rich.

Using his wealth and influence, Jones led successful fights against the law preventing free blacks from moving into Illinois, the "Black Laws," and school segregation in Chicago. Before the Civil War, he was active in the abolitionist movement and allowed his home to be used as a station on the Underground Railroad.

In 1875, Jones was elected to the Cook County board of commissioners and served for two terms. He was also the first black elected to the Chicago Board of Education. When he died in 1879, Jones left behind an estate worth more than $100,000.

January 11. With his armies almost ready to collapse, Robert E. Lee recommended using blacks in the Confederate forces because it was "not only expedient but necessary."

March 3. The U.S. Congress established a Bureau of Freedmen, Refugees and Abandoned Lands. Its job was to provide basic health and educational services to newly freed blacks and oversee abandoned land in the South.

During its five years of existence, the Freedmen's Bureau passed out food to hungry blacks and whites, established hospitals, set up schools, and resettled people who had lost their homes as a result of the war. It also played a role in the founding of black colleges such as Atlanta University, Fisk University, Hampton Institute, and Howard University.

March 3. The U.S. government authorized the formation of the Freedmen's Bank to encourage former slaves to manage their money wisely.

On April 4, 1865, the headquarters of the Freedmen's Bank opened in New York. Not long after, branches opened in Louisville, Kentucky; Nashville, Tennessee; New Orleans, Louisiana; Vicksburg, Mississippi; and Washington, D.C. By 1872 there were thirty-four branches, all but two of which were located in the South.

But the future of the Freedmen's Bank soon was in doubt due to incompetent and inefficient managers. By the time Frederick Douglass became its president in March, 1874, the bank was already a failure. It closed its doors on June 28, 1874.

March 13. Confederate President Jefferson Davis signed a bill that allowed blacks to serve as soldiers in the Confederate Army.

The new law ended a long fight in the South over the use of blacks as soldiers. While southerners had no problem using blacks behind the lines and as personal servants, they generally could not accept them as combat soldiers. The whites thought it made a joke out of the idea that blacks were inferior. They also feared that giving weapons to slaves might lead to violent uprisings.

The war ended before any blacks could fight for the South.

April 9. At the Appomattox Court House in Virginia, Confederate General Robert E. Lee formally surrendered to Union General Ulysses S. Grant. Within several days, the fighting had completely stopped across the country, finally bringing an end to the Civil War.

The assassination of Abraham Lincoln

April 14. President Abraham Lincoln was shot by John Wilkes Booth during a performance at Ford's Theater in the nation's capital. Lincoln died early the next morning. On April 26, Union soldiers tracked Booth to a barn in Virginia, where he was shot and killed after he refused to surrender.

May 29. The country's new president, Andrew Johnson, announced his program for Reconstruction, the process of reorganizing and rebuilding the southern states so that they could rejoin the Union. The program required Congress to ratify, or approve, the Thirteenth Amendment to the Constitution, which outlawed slavery and involuntary servitude (except as punishment for a crime). Johnson's program for reconstruction did not guarantee that blacks would one day have the right to vote, however.

December 18. Congress ratified (approved) the Thirteenth Amendment to the Constitution. It outlawed slavery in the United States.

All-white legislatures, acting under the Johnson Reconstruction program, began passing "Black Codes" that restricted the rights and freedom of movement of blacks. These new laws were modeled after the slave codes that had existed before the Civil War. They included strong punishments for roaming the streets, giving speeches intended to stir up people, making "insulting gestures," and violating curfew.

1866

January 9. Fisk University, one of the most prestigious black colleges in the nation, opened in Nashville, Tennessee.

April 9. The U.S. Congress passed the Civil Rights Bill of 1866 despite President Johnson's veto. This bill granted to blacks the rights and privileges of American citizenship and formed the basis for the Fourteenth Amendment to the Constitution. (Also see entry dated July 28, 1868.)

May 1-3. A race riot took place in Memphis, Tennessee. Forty-eight people, mostly black, died as a result of the disturbances. Black veterans were special targets, and at least five black women were raped. Rioters also burned schools and churches.

July 30. A race riot erupted in New Orleans, Louisiana. At least thirty-five people were killed. The violence allegedly stemmed from anti-black attitudes and actions on the part of police officers.

Edward G. Walker and Charles L. Mitchell became the first blacks to serve in an American legislative assembly when they were elected to the Massachusetts House of Representatives.

1867

January 8. The U.S. Congress passed a law giving the vote to blacks in the District of Columbia.

February 7. A delegation of blacks led by Frederick Douglass visited President Andrew Johnson and urged that the vote be given to all blacks who met the requirements laid down by their own states in connection with such things as sex, age, landownership, and literacy.

February 18. An institution was founded at Augusta, Georgia, which later became Morehouse College. Now located in Atlanta, Morehouse College is one of the most distinguished black colleges in the nation.

March 2. The U.S. Congress began passing a series of Reconstruction Acts that paved the way for blacks to participate in politics in the South. Before they could rejoin the Union, the former Confederate states had to ratify the Fourteenth Amendment, which guaranteed civil rights to blacks. (Also see entry dated July 28, 1868.)

April 1. The Ku Klux Klan, a violent anti-black group, held it first national convention in Nashville, Tennessee.

May 1. Howard University, "the capstone of Negro education," opened in Washington, D.C.

Atlanta University received its charter, or official approval to establish itself. It began as an undergraduate school but became the first all-black American graduate school in 1929.

The National Association of Baseball denied admission to any club with black players. In its official statement, the association declared: "If colored clubs were admitted, there would be in all probability some division of feeling—whereas by excluding them, no injury could result to anybody."

1868   **January 14.** The new state constitutional conventions met in Charleston, South Carolina. A large number of blacks were among the representatives whose job was to write new constitutions for the former Confederate states. Their spirit is reflected in the words of black representative Beverly Nash: "I believe, my friends and fellow-citizens, we are not prepared for this suffrage. But we can learn.... We recognize the Southern white man as the true friend of the black man.... In these public affairs we must unite with our white fellow-citizens. They tell us that they have been disfranchised, yet we tell the North that we shall never let the halls of Congress be silent until we remove that disability."

The state constitutions these southern delegates drew up stressed liberal reforms. They outlawed slavery on a state-by-state basis, made it illegal to put people in prison for being in debt, and insisted that people who wanted to vote or hold office did not have to own property.

April. Hampton Institute opened in Virginia. Once the country's leading agricultural-industrial training school for blacks, Hampton Institute remains one of the most prestigious black colleges in the United States.

June 7. Marie Laveau, the "Queen of the Voodoos," was forced to give up her throne because of old age.

Laveau was born free in New Orleans around 1796. She was a beautiful woman of mixed racial heritage who worked as a professional hairdresser in the homes of some of the city's most prominent white women.

Under Laveau's leadership, Louisiana Voodooism blended a distorted form of Catholicism with West Indian beliefs in the magical powers of certain objects. This unusual mixture made the cult very popular and helped it gain acceptance. Laveau's main source of power was her ability to convince blacks and whites that she could bring them good luck and protect them from evil. She dominated Voodooism in New Orleans for nearly forty years, becoming the most famous and powerful of all the Voodoo queens. Laveau died in 1879.

June 13. Oscar J. Dunn, a freedman, became lieutenant governor of Louisiana. At that time, it was the highest elective office ever held by a black American.

Dunn was born in New Orleans, Louisiana, in 1826. He worked as an apprentice to a plasterer and house painter until he was fifteen, when he escaped. During the Civil War, he served as a captain in the Union Army.

After the war, Dunn took a job with the Freedman's Bureau back in his hometown of New Orleans. He was also one of the forty-nine blacks who attended the Louisiana Constitutional Convention of 1867-1868. Later, as lieutenant governor, he led the state senate and signed some of the laws that grew out of the new state constitution. In 1871, Dunn became chairman of the Republican State Convention. A skillful politician, he was also mentioned as a possible candidate for governor or U.S. senator. But Dunn died later that same year before such plans could take shape.

Besides Dunn, two other blacks, C.C. Antoine and P.B.S. Pinchback, served as lieutenant governors of Louisiana. (See entries dated 1872 and March 8, 1876.) Blacks served as Reconstruction lieutenant governors in Mississippi and South Carolina as well.

July 6. The South Carolina Legislature met in Columbia, the state's capital. Of the 127 members, 87 were black, making South Carolina the only state legislature in American history to have a black majority.

Whites controlled the South Carolina State Senate, however, and by 1874 they also controlled the House of Representatives. At all times there was a white governor. There were two black lieutenant governors, Alonzo J. Ransier in 1870 and Richard H. Gleaves in 1872. Two blacks, Samuel J. Lee and Robert B. Elliot, served as Speaker of the House between 1872 and 1874.

One of the most talented black officeholders in South Carolina was Francis L. Cardozo. Educated in London, England, and Glasgow, Scotland, Cardozo served with distinction as secretary of state (1868-1872) and state treasurer (1872-1876).

July 28. The U.S. Congress ratified, or approved, the Fourteenth Amendment to the U.S. Constitution. This amendment stated that all people born in the United States were American citizens as well as citizens of the states in which they lived. (It also covered naturalized people—that is, people born outside the United States who had applied for and won citizenship.) The amendment said that no state could make or enforce laws denying such people the rights and privileges of citizens or fail to give them the equal protection of the laws.

Under the terms of the Fourteenth Amendment, blacks were finally considered American citizens with certain constitutional guarantees.

September 22-October 26. A series of race riots broke out in Louisiana. Disturbances occurred in New Orleans on September 22, in Opelousas on September 28, and in St. Bernard Parish on October 26.

1870　　**February 2.** Jonathan Jasper Wright, a native of Pennsylvania, became associate justice of the South Carolina Supreme Court. He served for seven years as the highest black judicial officer in the nation.

Although he did not have any influence on issues related to the rights of blacks, Wright was constantly the target of white Democrats who tried to force him off the bench with charges of corruption. He finally stepped down in 1877 as Reconstruction collapsed in the state.

February 25. Hiram R. Revels of Mississippi became the first black in the U.S. Congress when he took Jefferson Davis's former seat in the Senate. Many Democrats had tried to block his selection by arguing that he had not been a citizen before the Civil War. (According to the Constitution, a person cannot legally be a senator until he or she has been a citizen of the United States for at least nine years.)

Revels, a former barber and preacher, was a reluctant politician who left behind a mediocre record. He later became president of Alcorn College for Negroes in Mississippi. Revels died January 16, 1901, in Holly Springs, Mississippi.

March 30. The U.S. Congress ratified the Fifteenth Amendment to the Constitution. It said that American citizens could not be denied the right to vote because of their race, color, or previous status as a slave.

May 31, 1870-October 17, 1871. The U.S. Congress and President Ulysses S. Grant took steps to prevent whites from trying to frighten blacks away from the voting booth. The Enforcement Acts (also known as the Ku Klux Klan Acts) and a presidential proclamation were their most important efforts.

December 12. Joseph H. Rainey of South Carolina became the first black in the U.S. House of Representatives.

Rainey was born to slave parents of mixed racial heritage in Georgetown, South Carolina, in 1832. His father, a barber, purchased his son's freedom before the Civil War. Rainey himself became a barber in Charleston and learned much from listening to and observing his better-educated, white customers.

Even though he was a respected member of the local black community, Rainey was called on to help build Confederate fortifications during the Civil War. He refused and fled to the West Indies, where he remained until the end of the war.

During Reconstruction, Rainey returned to South Carolina and served as a delegate to the Constitutional Convention of 1868. In 1870 he was elected to the state senate

The first African American members of the U.S. Senate and House of Representatives (Hiram Revels is at far left)

but soon resigned to accept a vacant seat in the U.S. House of Representatives. Over the years, voters elected him to four more terms.

As a member of the House, Rainey often spoke out in favor of education and other social advances for blacks. He also served as a consultant to President Rutherford B. Hayes.

After leaving Congress in 1879, Rainey served as an Internal Revenue Service (IRS) agent in South Carolina and then went into business in Washington, D.C. He returned to Georgetown, South Carolina, in 1886 and died there a year later.

1872   Louisiana Lieutenant Governor P.B.S. Pinchback became the first black to serve as governor of an American state.

Pinchback was the son of a white Mississippi planter and army officer whose relationship with a woman of mixed racial heritage produced ten children. The father took all of his children north to obtain their freedom. Young Pinchback received private tutoring at home and then formal schooling in Cincinnati, Ohio.

After his father's death, Pinchback became a cabin boy on Mississippi river boats. During the Civil War, he organized a company of Union volunteers at New Orleans, Louisiana, and served as their captain.

Pinchback held several different political offices during the Reconstruction period, including that of United States senator from Louisiana. In the process, he earned a reputation as a clever and aggressive politician. His brief stint as governor of Louisiana came while he was serving as the state's lieutenant governor. For forty-three days, Pinchback sat in the governor's chair while the governor fought impeachment, or charges of wrongdoing. (Also see entry dated March 8, 1876.)

1873   **November.** The first black graduate of Harvard University, Richard T. Greener, was appointed to the faculty of the University of South Carolina. White students and faculty then left the college in protest.

1874   **July 31.** Father Patrick Francis Healy, a black priest, became president of Georgetown University, the oldest Catholic college in the United States. He headed the university until 1883. Healy was the brother of James Augustine Healy, the first black American to become a Roman Catholic bishop. (See entry dated April 6, 1830.)

1875   **March 1.** The U.S. Congress passed a civil rights bill that outlawed discrimination in public places such as hotels and theaters. It also banned it on forms of public transportation such as railroads and boats. But poverty and legal loopholes prevented most blacks from taking advantage of the new law, known as the Civil Rights Act of 1875. Eight years later, the U.S. Supreme Court overturned it. (Also see entry dated October 15, 1883.)

March 15. Mississippi's second black senator, Blanche K. Bruce, took his seat in the U.S. Congress. He was the only African American to serve a full term in the Senate until the mid-twentieth century.

Bruce was born a slave in Virginia. As the personal servant of a wealthy planter's son, he went along with his young master into the Confederate Army during the Civil War. Bruce managed to escape while they were in Missouri, where he established a school for blacks. He later attended Oberlin College for two years.

After the Civil War, Bruce became a modestly wealthy planter in Mississippi. He also taught school occasionally and held minor political offices as a Republican before being elected to the U.S. Senate. At the time of that election, Bruce's good reputation even managed to win him a few votes from white Democrats in the Mississippi legislature. But one white in particular was not at all impressed—his fellow senator from Mississippi. When it was time for Bruce to be sworn into office, his white colleague ignored custom and refused to escort him to the ceremony. So Senator Roscoe Conkling of New York took the black man's hand and led him to the front of the chamber. The historic moment received a great deal of publicity. (Also see entries dated May 19, 1881, and March 17, 1898.)

1876　　**March 8.** After three years of debate and controversy, members of the U.S. Senate refused to allow P.B.S. Pinchback of Louisiana to take his seat.

Pinchback had been elected to the U.S. House of Representatives in the fall of 1872. (See entry dated 1872.) Later, during the winter of 1873, he was elected to the U.S. Senate. Over the course of the long debate concerning his case, he became a national political figure as well as a prominent name in Washington society.

Senators who opposed Pinchback argued that he had not been properly elected to office or that he was not qualified. However, some historians believe that it was actually the senators' wives who influenced their husbands' votes against him. They were apparently upset at the thought of having to mix socially with Mrs. Pinchback.

Physicist Edward A. Bouchet received a Doctor of Philosophy degree from Yale University. It was the first such degree to be awarded to an African American by a major university.

July 8-October 26. President Ulysses S. Grant sent federal troops to South Carolina to restore order after serious racial disturbances erupted. In the town of Hamburg, five blacks were killed during the month of July.

The first all-black medical school in the United States, Meharry Medical College, was established in Nashville, Tennessee, as part of Central Tennessee College. It became an independent institution in 1915.

1877   **February 26.** Representatives of Republican presidential candidate Rutherford Hayes met with southern Democrats in Washington, D.C., to settle the controversial presidential election of 1876.

Hayes's Democratic opponent, Samuel Tilden, had actually won the most popular votes by a narrow margin (less than 170,000) and even led in the electoral college by a vote of 184-165. (The electoral college is a group of representatives from all of the states who meet after a presidential election and officially select the president and vice-president. Usually, their vote reflects exactly what the people of each state have already decided in the general election.) But as a result of fraud and violence in Louisiana, South Carolina, and Florida, the Hayes-Tilden election results were in doubt. A total of twenty electoral votes were at stake, enough to turn Hayes's defeat into victory.

After months of arguing, the two political parties reached a complicated agreement. The Democrats supported Hayes's election as president in exchange for several promises from the Republicans. The most important one involved removing the last federal troops who were supporting the government's Reconstruction policies in the South. Once those troops left, Reconstruction quickly came to an end.

March 18. Despite facing opposition within his own party as well as throughout most of the South, President Rutherford Hayes named Frederick Douglass marshal, or head law officer, for the District of Columbia.

1879   Large numbers of Southern blacks, frustrated with discrimination and poverty in the South, headed West (mostly to Kansas) in what came to be known as the "Exodus of 1879."

The best-known leader of the movement was Benjamin "Pap" Singleton. He was an uneducated former slave who, after a number of unsuccessful attempts, finally made his way to freedom in Canada. He favored racial separatism and encouraged blacks to become self-sufficient through hard work. Many better-educated African Americans rejected his idea of creating black communities apart from white influence.

1881   **April 11.** Spelman College for black women opened in Atlanta, Georgia. Sponsored by John D. Rockefeller's family, it became "the Radcliffe and the Sarah Lawrence of Negro education."

May 17. President James Garfield named Frederick Douglass recorder of deeds for the District of Columbia. It was Douglass's second important appointment to a government job.

May 19. President James Garfield appointed former Mississippi senator Blanche K. Bruce Register of the Treasury. (Also see entries dated March 15, 1875, and March 17, 1898.)

July 4. Booker T. Washington opened the famed Tuskegee Institute in Alabama. The school eventually became the leading African American agricultural and industrial school.

Tennessee became the first state to require that railroad cars be segregated. By 1907, all of the southern states had laws requiring segregation in public accommodations.

1883

March 20. Jan E. Matzeliger, a black Massachusetts shoemaker, invented a complicated shoe manufacturing machine that revolutionized the industry.

The son of a black woman and a Dutch engineer, Matzeliger was born in Paramaribo, Dutch Guiana, in 1852. He began working in his father's machine shop at the age of ten. Later, he worked his way to the United States as a sailor.

After a brief stay in Philadelphia, Pennsylvania, Matzeliger moved to Lynn, Massachusetts, where he learned the shoemaking trade. By 1880, machines were able to cut and stitch the leather but could not shape and attach the upper portion of the shoe to the sole. This had to be done by hand in a slow and tedious process called "lasting."

Working in secret for ten years, Matzeliger tried to invent a way to make the process faster and easier. In 1883, he received the patent for a "lasting machine" that could hold the shoe, grip and pull the leather down around the heel, set and drive the nails, and release the completed shoe. Matzeliger died in 1889.

October 15. The U.S. Supreme Court ruled that the Civil Rights Act of 1875 was unconstitutional. The act had made it illegal to discriminate in public places such

Sojourner Truth

as hotels and theaters and on forms of public transportation such as railroads and boats. According to the justices, the act was unconstitutional because the Reconstruction Amendments did not apply to the area of public accommodations. (Also see entry dated March 1, 1875.)

November 26. Sojourner Truth, the well-known black female abolitionist, died in Battle Creek, Michigan.

Born a slave in Hurley, New York, in 1797, she was originally named Isabella. Changes in New York state laws set her free in 1827. By then, she was the mother of five children but was separated from her husband. So she went to work in New York City for a man named Pierson who led a religious movement. By 1843, she had become disillusioned with Pierson and left his movement, proclaiming that her name was no longer Isabella, but Sojourner, which means "traveler." She said that "the Lord gave [her] Truth, because [she] was to declare the truth to the people."

Sojourner Truth then traveled around promoting abolition, women's rights, and other reforms. She firmly believed that she was a chosen messenger of God. Although she was not an educated woman, Truth made a strong impression on her audiences. On one occasion, when Frederick Douglass was speaking at Faneuil Hall in Boston, Massachusetts, he said that blacks could not hope to find justice in America. Truth responded to this pessimistic remark by asking, "Frederick, is God dead?" A more hopeful atmosphere then spread throughout the meeting.

During the Civil War, Truth supported the idea of giving weapons to slaves so that they could fight. She also helped care for wounded soldiers and freedmen. After the war and until the end of her life, she advised her audiences that the keys to black advancement were education and owning property.

1884   Black journalist T. Thomas Fortune published the first issue of a new newspaper, the *New York Age.*

Fortune was born in Florida in 1856 to parents of mixed racial heritage. After the

Civil War, he attended a Freedmen's Bureau school and worked as a page, or messenger, in the Florida state senate. (His father, a tanner and shoe merchant, served several terms in the Florida legislature during Reconstruction.) The family's political activities and close social contacts with some whites eventually created racial conflicts with other whites in Tallahassee. The Fortunes were finally forced to move to Jacksonville, where the father became town marshal.

Meanwhile, T. Thomas Fortune went on to Washington, D.C., where he attended Howard University. He helped pay for his education by working as a special customs agent in Delaware. After leaving Howard, he taught briefly in Florida but soon left for New York City.

In 1879, Fortune began his long newspaper career in New York City. His first job was with the *New York Sun,* one of the city's leading newspapers. He then went on to found his own paper and become the most prominent black journalist in the country until the time of the First World War. Fortune also published three books—

the well-known *Black and White* (1884), a historical essay on land, labor, and politics in the South, *The Negro in Politics* (1885), and *Dreams of Life* (1905).

In addition, Fortune played an active role in politics and civil rights. After the Civil War, for example, he supported the Republicans and closely identified with Booker T. Washington and his ideas. In his later years, however, he edited some of Marcus Garvey's black nationalist publications. During World War I, Fortune also helped establish the 369th black regiment. He died in 1928.

T. Thomas Fortune

1890   **August 12-November 1.** A constitutional convention in Mississippi approved an amendment that denied nearly all blacks the right to vote. The amendment included several ways in which officials could find a black person ineligible to vote. For example, it required blacks to pass certain literacy and "understanding" tests. It also established a poll tax of two dollars, meaning that those who could not afford to pay were not allowed to vote. Also banned from voting were blacks who had been convicted of bribery, burglary, theft, arson, murder, bigamy, and perjury.

Before the convention, black delegates from forty Mississippi counties had met and protested to President Benjamin Harrison about the pending loss of their right to vote, but the president refused to interfere. To avoid a long fight over ratification, the whites who supported the amendment declared it to be in effect as soon as the convention delegates approved it.

1891   **January 22.** The Lodge Bill, which was intended to prevent new laws from interfering with blacks' right to vote, was struck down in the U.S. Senate.

July 10. A black jockey, "Monk" Overton, won six straight horse races at the Washington Park race track in Chicago, Illinois. In 1907, another black jockey, Jimmy Lee, also won six straight races at Churchill Downs in Louisville, Kentucky. Prior to 1907, only two other jockeys in the world—Englishmen Fred Archer and George Fordham—had equalled the achievements of Overton and Lee.

Isaac Murphy, a black jockey riding "Kingman," became the first man to win three Kentucky Derbys. Murphy won his first Derby in 1884 on "Buchanan" and his second in 1890 on "Riley." Nine other black jockeys won the Derby a total of eleven times between 1875 and 1902.

1892   The Populist Party became an active political organization in the South. It appealed mostly to farmers and farm-related groups and welcomed black support at first. Populists favored more political power for ordinary voters and stronger regulation of big business.

Sissieretta Jones, a soprano nicknamed the "Black Patti," performed for President Benjamin Harrison at the White House.

Sissieretta Jones

Jones was born in Virginia, spent her childhood in Providence, Rhode Island, and studied at the New England Conservatory. She first attracted attention in 1892 when she appeared at the Jubilee Spectacle and Cakewalk at Madison Square Garden in New York City. One critic there called her the "Black Patti" after the Italian opera singer Adelina Patti.

According to some historians, officials from the Metropolitan Opera tried to sign up Jones for roles in *Aida* and *L'Africaine*. But they had to drop the idea, reportedly because some people in the musical world could not accept a black opera singer. Instead, Jones toured Europe in 1893. Upon her return to the United States, she organized an all-black company, "Black Patti's Troubadours," in which she was the featured soloist. She died in 1933.

1895   **February 20.** Frederick Douglass died in Washington, D.C. (Also see entries dated December 3, 1847; March 18, 1877; and May 17, 1881.)

September 18. Booker T. Washington, the head of Alabama's Tuskegee Institute, delivered his controversial "Atlanta Compromise" speech to the Cotton States International Exposition in Atlanta, Georgia. In his speech, he urged blacks to set aside their fight for political power and social equality and concentrate instead on making economic and educational progress. Washington also asked whites to help blacks in their efforts to become productive citizens. He reasoned that once blacks could show how important they were to the American economy, grateful whites would certainly grant them equal rights.

Washington had been born into slavery on a Virginia plantation in 1856. He later graduated from the Hampton Institute, a well-known black college that emphasized training in practical skills. In 1881, he was hired to establish and head a similar school in Tuskegee, Alabama. By the end of the decade, the Tuskegee Institute had earned praise from educators and business leaders around the entire nation for

Booker T. Washington

stressing that blacks could achieve economic success through self-help programs.

Washington himself was well on his way to becoming the best known and most respected black man in America by the time he was invited to speak at the Cotton States International Exposition. Five years later, he became even more famous when he published his autobiography, *Up from Slavery*. Southern and northern whites applauded its "reasonable" and forgiving attitude toward the South and the old slave system. The book is considered an American classic because of Washington's historical importance. (Also see entries dated August 23-24, 1900; October 16, 1901; July 11-13, 1905; June, 1906; and November 14, 1915.)

1896   **May 18.** The U.S. Supreme Court upheld the idea of "separate-but-equal" public facilities for blacks in the case of *Plessy v. Ferguson.*

The case grew out of a disagreement that occurred in Louisiana when a black railroad passenger named Homer Plessy refused to move out of a whites-only car. Plessy was arrested and challenged the state law allowing separate railroad cars for whites and blacks. A Louisiana judge ruled against him, and Plessy appealed to the U.S. Supreme Court, which also ruled against him.

The Supreme Court justices decided that it was "reasonable" for a state law to order that accommodations for blacks on a railway coach could be separate from those for whites as long as they were "equal." In their ruling, the Justices agreed that the fourteenth amendment to the Constitution had guaranteed certain rights to blacks. (See entry dated July 28, 1868.) They insisted, however, that the amendment "could not have been intended to abolish distinctions based on color, or to enforce social... equality, or (to bring about a mixing) of the two races upon terms unsatisfactory to either."

In showing its support for the Louisiana law, the nation's highest court approved the idea of legal racial segregation. In the statement he wrote opposing the Supreme Court's decision, Justice John Harlan correctly predicted that such segregation laws would just lead to more attacks against the rights of blacks. He also said that they encouraged ideas about racial inferiority.

July 21. Mary Church Terrell established the National Association of Colored Women (NACW) in Washington, D.C.

A native of Memphis, Tennessee, Terrell was born Mary Church in 1863. Her parents were wealthy and well educated and saw to it that their daughter was, too. She attended Oberlin College and probably would have become a teacher, but her father considered that occupation too ordinary for a young woman of her background. Instead, she married Robert Terrell, a prominent Washington, D.C., educator, attorney, and judge.

Terrell then became a leader in the fight for women's rights. She was also active in the battle against racial segregation. During the early 1950s, for example, Terrell—by then nearly ninety years old—headed a group of Washington blacks who demanded that officials enforce an old law banning restaurants from discriminating against customers on the basis of race or color as long as they were "well behaved." (See entry dated May 24, 1951.) On June 8, 1953, the U.S. Supreme Court upheld the old law. This decision opened the door to integrating other public facilities in Washington. Terrell died a year later on July 24, 1954.

Mary Church Terrell

1898   **March 17.** Former U.S. Senator Blanche K. Bruce died in Washington, D.C. After leaving the Senate, he had served as register of the U.S. Treasury and also was a successful banker. (Also see entries dated March 15, 1875, and May 19, 1881.)

April. Spain and the United States declared war on each other over the issue of Cuban independence. Approximately twenty black regiments ended up serving in the conflict, known as the Spanish-American War.

Blacks had continued to serve in the army after the Civil War, when regiments of so-called "Buffalo Soldiers" were drafted to fight out west against the Indians. But like many white soldiers, they were poorly prepared in terms of experience, equipment, and training for combat in a tropical zone like Cuba. Yet they won praise from almost all of their officers.

The Spanish-American War also led to promotions for many blacks. At the beginning of the conflict, for example, the army had only one black officer, Captain

The U.S. Tenth Colored Cavalry charges up San Juan Hill during the Spanish-American War

Charles Young. By the time it ended, however, there were more than 100 black officers.

July. At least twenty-five black soldiers, members of the U.S. Tenth Colored Cavalry, accompanied Theodore Roosevelt and his Rough Riders in the famous charge up San Juan Hill in Cuba. It was one of the major attacks of the Spanish-American War.

New York City's first black musical-comedy show, *Clorindy, the Origin of the Cakewalk,* opened on Broadway at the Casino Roof Garden. (The Cakewalk is a type of dance.)

Clorindy's creator and director was Will Marion Cook. A native of Washington, D.C., whose father was a Howard University law professor, Cook was born in 1869. As a teenager, he began studying the violin at the Oberlin Conservatory. He later studied with the violinist Joseph Joachim in Berlin, Germany, and with musician John White and composer Antonin Dvorak at the National Conservatory of Music.

Ignoring warnings that Broadway audiences would not listen to blacks singing black opera, Cook developed *Clorindy* by composing music to go along with lyrics written by famous black poet Paul Laurence Dunbar. (See entry dated February 9, 1906.) He then assembled a group of twenty-six black performers to sing and act in the show.

After *Clorindy* became a hit, Cook continued to make theatrical history with other works, including *In Dahomey* (1902), a satire on the American Colonization Movement's efforts to promote black emigration to Africa, *In Abyssinia* (1906), and *In Bandana Land* (1907). His lively shows left audiences whistling and tapping their feet and helped to popularize the Cakewalk in the United States and Europe. Cook died in 1944.

1899   Charles Waddell Chesnutt published a book of stories based on the superstitions of North Carolina blacks. Called *The Conjure Woman,* it helped establish him as the leading African American novelist of his time.

Chesnutt was born in North Carolina in 1858 but spent much of his adult life in Ohio. For several years after the Civil War, however, he taught in the public schools of North Carolina and then became principal of the Fayetteville State Teachers

College. As segregation and discrimination grew worse throughout the South during the 1880s, Chesnutt returned to the North. He settled first in New York, where he worked as a journalist. He then moved to Cleveland, Ohio, where he was a clerk and an attorney.

Before publishing *The Conjure Woman*, Chesnutt contributed several short stories to American magazines, including the *Atlantic Monthly*. Following the tremendous success of *The Conjure Woman*, which many consider to be his best work, he published *The*

Charles Waddell Chesnutt

Wife of His Youth (1900), *The House behind the Cedars* (1900), *The Marrow of Tradition* (1901), and *The Colonel's Dream* (1905).

In recognition of his literary and other achievements, the National Association for the Advancement of Colored People (NAACP) awarded Chesnutt its prestigious Spingarn Medal in 1928. He died in 1932.

1900   **April 30.** The famous steam locomotive driven by John "Casey" Jones collided with another train in a deadly crash that has become part of American folklore thanks to a song.

Among the members of Jones's crew on that fateful day were two black men, Wallace Saunders and Sim Webb. Just before the crash, Jones ordered Webb to jump to safety while he himself remained on board. When authorities found Jones's body, they saw that he had kept one hand on the brake and the other on the whistle until the very end.

The accident inspired Saunders to honor the brave engineer with a song—the popular tune entitled "Casey Jones."

July 24-27. A serious race riot broke out in New Orleans, Louisiana. Black schools and homes were destroyed during the disturbance.

August 23-24. The National Negro Business League, sponsored by Booker T. Washington, was formed in Boston, Massachusetts.

More than 400 delegates from 34 states had answered Washington's call to encourage the development of black businesses. Washington himself was elected the first president of the organization. At the end of only one year, he reported a large increase in the number of new black businesses. By 1907, the national organization had 320 branches.

1901   **March 4.** North Carolina's George H. White left the U.S. House of Representatives after serving for two terms. More than twenty years would go by before any other African American served in Congress.

In a moving farewell speech to his colleagues, White attacked "Jim Crowism," a term often used to describe the many laws segregating the races in the South. (Jim Crow was a character in a popular song.) He also predicted that blacks would one day return to Congress.

October 16. Booker T. Washington had dinner with President Theodore Roosevelt at the White House. Many whites—especially southerners—bitterly criticized the meeting for going against social rules that looked down on such racial mixing.

William Monroe Trotter founded the *Boston Guardian,* a militant newspaper that opposed the policies of Booker T. Washington and demanded full equality for blacks.

Trotter was born in Boston, Massachusetts in 1872 and earned both a bachelor of arts and master's degree from Harvard University. To establish the *Guardian,* he gave up a promising career as an insurance executive. As he later noted: "The conviction grew upon me that pursuit of business, money, civic or literary position was like building a house upon sands; if race prejudice and persecution and public discrimination for mere color was to spread up from the South and result in a fixed caste of color ... every colored American would be really a civil outcast, forever an alien, in the public life."

One of the chief targets of his criticism was Booker T. Washington, head of Alabama's Tuskegee Institute. On July 30, 1903, Trotter and some of his followers were arrested for heckling the prominent black leader at the Columbus Avenue African Zion Church in Boston, Massachusetts. Trotter later explained that he had decided to face Washington publicly because he felt that American newspapers and magazines liked the "Tuskegee kingpin" so much they would not publish the views of people who disagreed with him. Trotter's arrest and eventual jail term inspired W.E.B. Du Bois to become active in the movement against Washington and his ideas.

Trotter remained devoted to the cause of equal rights throughout his entire life. In 1906, for example, he protested when President Theodore Roosevelt discharged the black soldiers involved in the Brownsville, Texas, riot. (See entry dated April 13, 1906.) In 1910, Trotter led a demonstration against a performance of the anti-black play *The Clansman* in Boston. In 1913 he confronted President Woodrow Wilson at the White House and accused him of lying when Wilson denied that he was responsible for segregating government cafeterias in Washington, D.C. Two years later, Trotter landed in jail for picketing the showing of the anti-black film *Birth of a Nation.* (See entry dated November 14, 1915.)

Eager to attend the Paris Peace Conference after World War I, Trotter applied for a passport so that he could go to France and present the complaints of American blacks to a worldwide audience. When the U.S. government refused to give him a passport, he got a job as a cook on a transatlantic ship and sailed to Europe. He finally made his way to the meeting as a representative of the National Equal Rights League and of the Race Petitioners to the Peace Conference. In this role, he supported a move by the Japanese to include a ban against discrimination in the charter of the newly formed League of Nations. But the western allies, including the United States, opposed including such a ban.

Even during his final years, with his money and his energy running out, Trotter kept up the fight. He died in 1934. (Also see entries dated 1903; July 11-13, 1905; and February 12, 1909.)

1903   Scholar and activist W.E.B. Du Bois published his essay collection, *The Souls of Black Folk.* In it he explained why he and others who felt as he did (including

W.E.B. Du Bois

William Monroe Trotter) opposed the policies of Booker T. Washington.

Du Bois was born in Great Barrington, Massachusetts, in 1868. His father was a restless man who left town within a year after his son's birth, forcing the young boy and his sickly mother to turn to relatives and neighbors for help. A brilliant student, Du Bois received bachelor's degrees from both Fisk University and Harvard University. He completed graduate studies at the University of Berlin, and in 1895 he became the first black to earn a doctorate degree from Harvard.

After teaching at Wilberforce University and the University of Pennsylvania, Du Bois became professor of history and economics at Atlanta University. He stayed there for twelve years and made the school a center for studies in black sociology (the study of society and social relationships between groups of people). Many of his findings were collected in *The Atlanta University Publications* (1898-1914). Along with *The Souls of Black Folk* and his earlier works, *The Suppression of the African Slave Trade to America* (1896) and *The Philadelphia Negro* (1899), *The Atlanta University Publications* helped establish his scholarly reputation.

During this same period, Du Bois also contributed many articles to major magazines and newspapers in which he harshly criticized the country's most popular black leader, Booker T. Washington. Du Bois totally rejected Washington's policies of compromise and accommodation, which urged blacks to put aside their desire for political and social equality and work instead to achieve economic success. These articles touched off a bitter public feud between the two men, especially after they appeared in *The Souls of Black Folk*.

Eventually, Du Bois banded together with fellow radical William Monroe Trotter and other anti-Washington blacks to develop a new type of black leadership. Their efforts led first to the Niagara Movement and later to the National Association for the Advancement of Colored People (NAACP).

Du Bois served the NAACP for some twenty-five years as editor of the *Crisis,* the group's official magazine, and as director of publications. His increasing political radicalism caused tension within the NAACP, however, and in 1934 Du Bois resigned to return to Atlanta University. He remained there until 1944, when he briefly worked for the NAACP again as head of its research department. In 1948, he was once again forced out of the organization after he angered NAACP leaders with his outspokenness.

Du Bois then ran for (and lost) a seat in the U.S. Senate as a candidate of the American Labor Party. During the 1950s, he also served as the head of several organizations that the U.S. government thought were trying to overthrow the country because they had ties to the Soviet Union. As a result, the police, the FBI, and the State Department harassed Du Bois—by then in his eighties—until he lost all hope that black Americans would ever know freedom in their own land. In 1961, he decided to move to Africa, where he settled in Ghana and worked as editor-in-chief of the *Encyclopedia Africana.* (Also see entries dated July 11-13, 1905; February 12, 1909; April, 1910; February 19-21, 1919; and August 27, 1963.)

1905　**July 11-13.** Led by W.E.B. Du Bois and William Monroe Trotter, a group of black intellectuals from across the nation met near Niagara Falls, New York, to discuss their opposition to Booker T. Washington. They ended their meeting by passing resolutions that demanded full equality for blacks in American life. The meeting has become known to history as the beginning of the Niagara Movement.

The Atlanta Life Insurance Company was founded by Alonzo F. Herndon in Atlanta, Georgia. It was once the largest black-owned business in the United States.

Robert Sengstacke Abbott began publishing the militant *Chicago Defender,* one of the most

Robert Sengstacke Abbott

widely read and influential black newspapers in the country.

Abbott was the son of a slave butler and a field woman who purchased their son's freedom. After her husband died, Mrs. Abbott married John Sengstacke, an editor, educator, and clergyman. Young Abbott worked on his stepfather's news sheet and received his education at the Hampton Institute.

Abbott established the *Defender* in Chicago, Illinois with a staff of former barbers and servants as well as a few recently educated blacks. He attracted good journalists like Willard Motley and also published the early poems of Gwendolyn Brooks. Abbott's brutal attacks on southern racism and his appeals to blacks to move north helped earn widespread respect for the *Defender*.

1906   **February 9.** Paul Laurence Dunbar, the black poet who made black dialect an accepted literary form, died in Dayton, Ohio.

The son of a former slave, Dunbar was born in Dayton in 1872. Although he was senior class poet at Dayton's Central High School and editor of the school newspaper and yearbook, Dunbar first worked as an elevator boy. In 1893 he compiled a book of his verse that he sold to passengers on his elevator.

Two years later, Dunbar published *Majors and Minors*. It brought him national attention after William Dean Howells wrote a very favorable review of the book in *Harper's Weekly*. Dunbar followed up his first success the next year with *Lyrics of Lowly Life*. (Many of his early works were published by airplane inventors Orville and Wilbur Wright, who were experimenting at the time with printing newspapers on a homemade press.) In 1897 Dunbar became an assistant at the Library of Congress, a position he held only a year.

During the last ten years of his life, Dunbar produced eleven volumes of poetry, three novels, and five collections of short stories. Even though he was from the Midwest, he wrote about the Old South with humor and a certain tenderness for days gone by.

No black writer before him had been so widely praised by white and black Americans. Critics generally agree that his best work is his poetry, especially the ones written in black dialect. William Dean Howells, for example, thought Dunbar was the first African American to have an artist's appreciation for the life of his people that he expressed in verse. Dunbar's biographer, Benjamin Brawley, said that Dunbar "soared above race and touched the heart universal. He came on the scene at a time when America was being launched on the machine age and when the country was beset with problems.... In a world of discord, he dared to sing his song about nights bright with stars, about the secret of the wind and the sea, and the answer one finds beyond the years. Above the dross and strife of the day, he asserted the right to live and love and be happy. That is why he was so greatly beloved and why he will never grow old."

The conflict between Dunbar's genius and the limitations he faced because of racism probably brought about his early death. He was only thirty-four when he died from the effects of alcoholism and tuberculosis.

April 13. Serious racial disturbances involving white civilians and black soldiers occurred at Brownsville, Texas, resulting in the deaths of at least three white men.

The trouble began when the whites taunted the black soldiers with racial slurs, and the black soldiers struck back. President Theodore Roosevelt responded by dishonorably discharging the black soldiers. This convinced many blacks that they could not count on him to take action against the increasing amount of racial violence aimed at blacks.

When the U.S. Congress met in December, 1906, some northerners, led by Senator Joseph B. Foraker of Ohio, protested that there should have been a full investigation and trial before the president discharged the black soldiers. A Senate committee launched such an investigation in January, 1907. After several months, the committee released a report supporting the president's decision. Finally, in 1909, Senator Foraker won approval for a court of inquiry to pass on the cases of the discharged soldiers and to allow all men judged eligible to reenlist.

June. John Hope assumed the presidency of Morehouse College.

One of the most militant of early black educators, Hope was the school's first African American president. He also was the man behind many of the programs that earned the school its reputation for excellence.

Hope was born in 1868 in Augusta, Georgia, to a white father and mother of mixed racial heritage. The family was quite prosperous, and young John's childhood was happy and secure until his father died in 1876. Then the actions of some prejudiced whites and cold-hearted executors (the people in charge of carrying out the terms of a will) caused the family to lose most of their money. That same year, young Hope witnessed a violent racial clash in Atlanta. This incident, together with the

Atlanta riot of 1906 (see entry dated September 22-24, 1906), probably helped make him into a radical.

Hope criticized Booker T. Washington's "Atlanta Compromise" speech (see entry dated September 18, 1895) and was the only black college president to join the militant Niagara Movement. He was also the only college administrator to attend the founding meeting of the NAACP (see entry dated February 12, 1909).

In 1919, Hope co-founded the South's first biracial reform group, the Commission on Interracial Cooperation. (It was the forerunner of the Southern Regional Council.) He served as the group's president beginning in 1932. Hope was also president of Atlanta University from 1929 until his death in 1936. That same year, the NAACP awarded him the Spingarn Medal for his achievements as an educational and civil rights leader.

September 22-24. A major race riot in Atlanta, Georgia, left twelve people dead. Racial tensions had been running high for quite some time, mostly due to irresponsible reporting in the city's newspapers and attempts to deny blacks the right to vote.

On September 22, the newspapers reported four successive assaults on white women by black men. Many of the city's whites, joined by country people in town for Saturday shopping, then formed mobs that went looking for revenge. Police quickly arrested blacks who tried to arm themselves in defense against the angry whites. The state of panic continued for several days until a group of blacks and whites held a meeting and asked people to calm down. Out of this sprang the Atlanta Civic League, an interracial organization dedicated to racial harmony.

1907   Alain Locke became the first black to receive a Rhodes Scholarship to study at England's Oxford University. No other black won this distinguished award for more than half a century.

Locke was born in Philadelphia in 1886. After completing his studies in England in 1910, he went on to the University of Berlin and earned a doctorate degree from Harvard University in 1918. He became professor of philosophy at Howard University in 1912, a position he held until he retired in 1953.

In 1916, Locke published *Race Contacts and Interracial Relations*. But his fame as a literary and art critic and interpreter of black culture rests largely on his anthology *The New Negro* (1925), a work about the Harlem Renaissance. Locke died before he could finish another one of his noteworthy books, *The Negro in American Culture*. It was completed by Margaret Just Butcher and published in 1956, two years after Locke's death.

1908

August 14-19. A serious racial disturbance occurred in Springfield, Illinois. The shock of having a riot take place near Abraham Lincoln's home caused concerned whites to call for a conference that led to the founding of the NAACP. (See entry dated February 12, 1909.)

December 26. Fighter Jack Johnson became the first nationally famous black heavyweight champion when he knocked out white boxer Tommy Burns.

Born in 1878 in Galveston, Texas, Johnson was the son of a school janitor. As a young man, he worked his way around the country as a stevedore, a person who loads and unloads cargo ships while they are in port. He learned how to box along the way by practicing with professional fighters whenever he had the chance.

Jack Johnson

Johnson's victory over Burns came nine years after he had begun to box. It touched off a bitter racial controversy because it involved a black man beating a white man. Boxing fans urged the former white champion, Jim Jeffries, to come out of retirement so that he could fight Johnson and recapture the title. When the two men finally met on July 4, 1910, Johnson kept his championship by knocking out Jeffries in the fourteenth round. Five years later, he lost it to another boxer and then retired from the ring.

Johnson died in a car accident in Raleigh, North Carolina, on June 10, 1946. His life and career later inspired a Broadway play and film, both of which are entitled *The Great White Hope*. Actor James Earl Jones played a character based on Johnson in both productions.

Matthew Alexander Henson

1909   **February 12.** The National Association for the Advancement of Colored People (NAACP), was founded in New York City. For many years, it was the nation's most important civil rights organization.

White liberals and black intellectuals were the group's first leaders. Among them were Jane Addams, John Dewey, W.E.B. Du Bois, Mary White Ovington, and Oswald Garrison Villard. Moorfield Storey of Boston, Massachusetts served as president. Black activist William Monroe Trotter refused to accept a leadership role because he distrusted whites.

April 6. Black explorer Matthew Alexander Henson and Admiral Robert E. Peary shared in the discovery of the North Pole.

Henson was born in Maryland in 1866, the son of free-born sharecroppers. Historians believe he was orphaned at an early age and ran away from home when he was about eleven to escape from a cruel stepmother.

Making his way to Washington, D.C., Henson moved in with an uncle and went to school for a while. He then worked as a cabin boy on board a merchant ship and later as a stock boy in a Washington clothing store. There he met Peary, who hired Henson as his personal servant.

Henson and Peary then went on several expeditions together, including one to Nicaragua and several to the Arctic in search of the exact location of the North Pole. Henson proved to be an expert guide and surveyor (a person who measures and maps land areas). After surviving many hardships, the two men finally reached their goal. Although Peary received almost all of the glory and fame, Henson may have actually been the first man to stand "on top of the world," as he later put it.

His career as an explorer at an end, Henson worked for many years as a messenger in the New York Customs House. He received almost no recognition for his part in the North Pole expedition until later in life, when he received several medals, including one from Congress for "outstanding service to the government of the United States in the field of science."

Henson died in 1955.

1910   **April.** The National Urban League (NUL) was established in New York City. Designed to help southern blacks who had moved to the North, it soon became a social relief organization for black city dwellers in the North, West, and later in the South.

The NAACP's official magazine, the *Crisis,* began publication with W.E.B. Du Bois serving as its first editor.

1912   **September 27.** A revolution in the music world occurred when W. C. Handy published his blues composition, "Memphis Blues."

1913   **March 10.** Harriet Tubman died in Auburn, New York. She was often described as the "Moses of her people" because she led so many slaves to freedom via the Underground Railroad in the years before the Civil War. (Also see entry dated July, 1849.)

1915   **September 9.** Professor Carter G. Woodson founded the Association for the Study of Negro Life and History (ASNLH). For many years, it was one of just a few groups that tried to show the real role of African Americans in U.S. history.

Woodson, the son of former slaves, held a doctorate degree from Harvard University. He edited a number of publications of the ASNLH, including the *Journal of Negro History.* He also wrote several books on African Americans. Because he was so interested in black history, Woodson is sometimes called "the father of modern Negro historiography," or the writing down of history. The

NAACP recognized his efforts in 1926 by awarding him a Spingarn Medal. He died April 3, 1950, in Washington, D.C.

November 14. Booker T. Washington died at Alabama's Tuskegee Institute.

Once the most famous and influential black American of his time, Washington had become much less powerful during the last few years of his life. Many blacks no longer believed that his conservative approach to race relations would make their lives better. Instead, they had begun looking to the NAACP for leadership. (Also see entries dated September 18, 1895; August 23-24, 1900; October 16, 1901; July 11-13, 1905; and June, 1906.)

November 14. The NAACP led the black outcry against the showing of D.W. Griffith's controversial film, *Birth of a Nation.*

Based on the racist writings of Thomas Dixon, *Birth of a Nation* was the most technologically advanced motion picture produced at that time. But it gave a distorted view of emancipation, Reconstruction, and black immorality. It also made heroes out of such anti-black organizations as the Ku Klux Klan.

November 14. Black Pan-Africanist leader and AME bishop Henry McNeal Turner died.

Turner was born free in Abbeville, South Carolina, in 1833. At an early age he was hired out to work in the field with slaves. His first lessons were from a white playmate.

Making his way to Baltimore, Maryland, at the age of fifteen, Turner worked as a messenger and a handyman at a medical school, where he had access to books and magazines. He continued his self-education until an Episcopal bishop agreed to teach him. This was one of the influences that led Turner to become an AME minister.

During the Civil War, President Lincoln appointed Turner chaplain of the 54th Massachusetts black regiment. After the war, he worked with the Freedmen's Bureau in Georgia and became actively involved in Republican politics. He served in the Georgia constitutional convention of 1868 and was elected to the state legislature, where he strongly opposed the successful attempt of white lawmakers to expel the Black Reconstruction legislators.

These and other experiences eventually convinced Turner that the black man had no future in the United States. He became a colonizationist and Pan-Africanist, or a supporter of the rights of native Africans and their descendants all over the world. In 1878, he was among the backers of a failed expedition involving about 200 blacks who went to Liberia hoping to settle there.

In addition to these activities, Turner served the AME Church in various ways. He was director of the AME publishing house and editor of the church's periodicals, for example, and was head of Morris Brown College, an AME school in Atlanta, Georgia.

1917   **April 16.** The United States entered World War I.

Approximately 300,000 blacks served during this conflict, and about 1,400 of them became officers. Three black regiments received the *croix de guerre,* a special military award given for bravery. Several individual blacks were also decorated for bravery.

July 1-3. A serious race riot occurred in East St. Louis, Illinois. At least forty blacks were killed, and the government called in military forces to help the local police maintain order.

The riot erupted after blacks were hired to work in a factory that had a contract with the federal government. In one of the most tragic incidents, a small black child was shot down and then thrown into a burning building.

The Germans, who had just gone to war with the United States, tried to use the riot to their advantage. They pointed to it as a reason for blacks to support Germany instead of the U.S. government.

July 28. About 10,000 blacks participated in a silent march down Fifth Avenue in New York City to protest racial oppression.

The march was organized by the NAACP in response to the East St. Louis riot earlier in the month. (See entry dated July 1-3, 1917.) The protestors encouraged everyone to pray for East St. Louis and asked President Woodrow Wilson, "Why not make America safe for democracy?" This was a reference to the "make the world safe for democracy" slogan Wilson had been using to inspire support for the war effort.

August 23. A serious disturbance between black soldiers and white civilians erupted in Houston, Texas. Two blacks and seventeen whites were killed. Thirteen blacks were later executed for participating in the riot.

November 5. Emmett J. Scott, former secretary to Booker T. Washington, was appointed special assistant to the Secretary of War.

Scott's job was to watch for signs of discrimination in the draft process, make plans to build up morale among blacks, soldiers, and civilians, and investigate complaints of unfair treatment of blacks. He also publicized news concerning black soldiers and related activities on the home front.

In June, 1918, Scott gathered together about thirty black newspaper publishers who pledged their support to the American war effort but criticized anti-black violence and discrimination at home. The group also encouraged the Red Cross to recruit black nurses, asked for the appointment of a black war correspondent, and called on the government to return retired black Colonel Charles Young to active duty. (See entry dated January 8, 1922.) Most of these requests were granted.

The NAACP awarded Harry T. Burleigh with its highest honor, the Spingarn Medal, for excellence in the field of creative music.

Burleigh was born in Erie, Pennsylvania, in 1866. Although he showed a talent for music as a child, he did not receive formal training until many years later. He began his studies in 1892 at the National Conservatory of Music in New York City, where he majored in orchestral as well as vocal music. During his sophomore year, he trained under the famous Czech composer Antonin Dvorak. Dvorak made a special effort to help the young black student develop his abilities.

Two years after entering the conservatory, Burleigh was well on his way to a singing career. He became the first black soloist at St. George's Episcopal Church in New York and at the Temple Emanu-El. His European tours included a command performance before King Edward VII in England. During his senior year, Burleigh became an instructor of voice at the Conservatory, a position he held for two years after his graduation.

Around 1900, however, Burleigh began to shift his attention from singing to composing. His first works were sentimental ballads. He then branched out into choral pieces, spirituals, and other kinds of music.

In all his compositions, Burleigh's goal was to capture and preserve the sound and spirit of black folk songs. Among his better known pieces are "Six Plantation Melodies for Violin and Piano" (1901), "The Prayer" (1915), "Southland Sketches" (1916), "Deep River" (1916), "Little Mother of Mine" (1917), and "The Lovely Dark and Lonely One" (1935).

Burleigh died in 1949.

1918   **July 13-October 1.** Major race riots occurred across the nation during what poet James Weldon Johnson called the "Red Summer."

More than 25 riots left over 100 people dead and more than 1,000 wounded. Federal troops had to put an end to the disorders in some instances. Among the places that experienced violence that summer were Washington, D.C., Chicago, Illinois, Longview, Texas, and the Pennsylvania cities of Chester and Philadelphia.

1919   **February 19-21.** The First Pan-African Congress, led by W.E.B. Du Bois, met in Paris, France. It ran at the same time as the Paris Peace Conference, which ended World War I. In attendance were about sixty delegates, including West Indians, Africans, and American blacks.

The meeting focused attention on the fact that blacks all over the world had a great deal of interest in the outcome of the Paris Peace Conference, especially in terms of how they might benefit from it. In their view, the democracy for which many of them had fought now needed to become a reality.

Marcus Garvey

While this first meeting accomplished very little, it inspired other meetings of black people in later years that proved to be more successful. In 1920, Du Bois received the NAACP's Spingarn Medal for his efforts to promote unity among blacks all over the world through the Pan-African Congress.

1920　　**August 1-2.** The national convention of the Universal Negro Improvement Association (UNIA), an organization of black nationalists, met in New York City. Marcus Garvey, the founder of UNIA, spoke to approximately 25,000 blacks during a rally at Madison Square Garden.

Garvey had begun his movement in 1914 in his native Jamaica. In 1916 he came to New York to organize a local chapter of UNIA. By the middle of 1919 there were thirty branches of the organization in the United States, mostly in northern ghettoes. Garvey founded a newspaper, the *Negro World,* to help spread his ideas about race pride and to promote his back-to-Africa program. He also established several offshoots of UNIA, including the Black Star Steamship Line.

In 1921, Garvey formally organized the Empire of Africa and appointed himself its temporary president. He appealed unsuccessfully to the League of Nations for permission to settle a colony in Africa and even talked with Liberian officials about the project. When this didn't work out, he began planning a military expedition to force white colonists off the continent. Such an attack was never launched, however.

In 1925, Garvey was sent to jail for mail fraud in connection with his attempts to raise money for his steamship line. Two years later, he was released from prison and deported (sent out of the country) as an undesirable alien. In the meantime, his black nationalist movement had fallen apart, and his efforts to revive it after he was free again failed.

Garvey died June 10, 1940, in London, England.

August. Robert Nathaniel Dett, black composer, arranger, and conductor, received Harvard University's Bowdoin Prize for an essay entitled "The Emancipation of Negro Music."

Dett was born in 1882 in the Canadian community of Drummondville, Quebec. It had been established by escaped slaves before the Civil War. Inspired as a child by black spirituals, Dett later studied music at the American Conservatory of Music in Chicago, Illinois, Columbia University, Harvard University, the Oberlin Conservatory, the Oliver Willis Halstead Conservatory in Lockport, New York, and the University of Pennsylvania. Early in his career, he also performed as a concert pianist.

Dett taught at a number of institutions, including Lane College in Texas (1908-11), Lincoln University in Missouri (1911-13), Hampton Institute in Virginia (1913-31), Sam Houston College in Texas (1935-37), and Bennett College in North Carolina (1937). Under his leadership, the Hampton Institute Choir became known throughout the world. He later took some time off to study with Arthur Foote in Boston, Massachusetts, and with Nadia Boulanger at the American Conservatory in Fontainebleau, France.

Among Dett's many notable compositions are *Magnolia* (five piano suites, 1912), *Music in the Mine* (1916), *The Chariot Jubilee* (oratorio, 1921), *Enchantment* (1922), and *The Ordering of Moses* (1937).

Dett died in 1943.

1921

Ragtime pianist and composer Eubie Blake, along with bandleader Noble Sissle, produced the historic musical *Shuffle Along.*

The son of former slaves, Blake was born in Baltimore, Maryland, in 1883. At the age of four, he wandered into a music store while his mother was shopping and began to play a pump organ. A salesman convinced his mother that the boy had talent, and she bought the $75 instrument. He learned about ragtime by following black funeral processions and imitating the lively tunes musicians played on the way back from the cemetery.

Eubie Blake in 1976

Like most young black musicians of his time, Blake began his career playing piano in brothels and gambling houses. In 1899, he composed his first ragtime piece, "The Charleston Rag." After 1915, he began working with Sissle, who served as his agent as well as his writing partner.

Shuffle Along, which featured the songs "I'm Just Wild about Harry" and "Love Will Find a Way," was one of the first black musicals to appear on Broadway. (In 1948, "I'm Just Wild about Harry" became Harry S. Truman's theme song during that year's presidential campaign.) It played for 504 performances and helped launch the careers of Josephine Baker, Florence Mills, Paul Robeson, and other entertainers. After finishing its successful run on Broadway, the show toured the country.

Another of Blake's shows, *Blackbirds,* became a big hit in 1930. It featured John Bubbles, Buck Washington, and Ethel Waters and such famous tunes as "Memories of You" and "You're Lucky to Me."

Blake's popularity began to fade during the Great Depression of the 1930s. The death of his wife in 1939 added to his feelings of despair. Then things began to look up for him. He played for American troops during the war, and in 1945 he married his second wife, who helped him put his personal life and business affairs back in order.

But it was not until ragtime became popular again in the 1960s that Blake reached a new generation of music lovers. Even then, at the age of nearly ninety, he was still composing rags as part of a major recording contract he signed with Columbia Records in 1969. (Also see entry dated February 12, 1983.)

1922   **January 8.** Colonel Charles R. Young, one of the highest-ranking blacks in the U.S. Army, died in the African country of Nigeria.

Young, the son of a former slave-soldier in the Union Army, was born in Kentucky. He entered West Point Academy in 1884 and served with distinction in Cuba, Haiti, and Mexico.

Racial discrimination always made Young's career a tough struggle, however. During World War I, he was called up for a physical examination and then retired due to "poor health." This was apparently a scheme to avoid promoting him to general. After blacks protested (see entry dated November 5, 1917), Young was recalled to active duty. But he was only allowed to serve in relatively minor positions in Illinois and Liberia.

A period of great achievement in African American art and literature known as the Harlem Renaissance began in New York City and ran throughout the rest of the 1920s. The writings of such poets as Claude McKay, Langston Hughes, Countee Cullen, James Weldon Johnson, and the novelists Walter F. White, Wallace Thurman, Nella Larsen, and Zora Neale Hurston, among others, received critical and popular praise from both blacks and whites. Among the notable artists of the era were sculptors Richmond Barthe and Augusta Savage, and painters Aaron Douglas, Alice Gafford, and Archibald Motley.

During the Harlem Renaissance, two important anthologies of the works of black writers were published—James Weldon Johnson's *The Book of American Negro Poetry* (1925) and Alain Locke's *The New Negro* (1925). Claude McKay, the first important figure in the Harlem Renaissance, was noted for his *Harlem Shadows* (1922), a collection of bitter but eloquent poems on the condition of blacks in postwar America. Countee Cullen's volume of poems entitled *Color* (1925) was another major achievement.

Other notable works published during this period were poet Langston Hughes's *The Weary Blues* (1926), Walter White's *The Fire in the Flint* (1926), Nella Larsen's *Quicksand* (1928) and *Passing* (1929), and Wallace Thurman's *The Blacker the Berry* (1929).

1923   **September 4.** George Washington Carver of Tuskegee Institute received the NAACP's Spingarn Medal for distinguished research in agricultural chemistry.

Carver was born a slave near Diamond Grove, Missouri, in late 1864 or early 1865. When

George Washington Carver

he was just a baby, he was kidnapped along with his mother from their master's farm and taken to Arkansas. A man hired by the master was able to track down young George and return him to Missouri, but his mother was never heard from again. So the master and his wife, who were childless, raised the orphaned George and his older brother as their own.

Carver went to local schools until he was about thirteen. Then he left Missouri and spent his teenage years restlessly wandering back and forth across several midwestern states. Along the way, he managed to finish high school, doing odd jobs such as sewing and laundry to support himself. He then enrolled in college and earned his bachelor's and master's degrees in agriculture from Iowa State College.

In 1896, Carver joined the faculty of the Tuskegee Institute in Alabama. There he began researching soil conservation and tried to convince southern farmers to branch out and grow crops other than cotton. (His fame as a scientist, in fact, stems largely from the 400 different products he showed could be produced from the peanut, potato, and pecan.) He also traveled across the South and talked with some of the region's poorest farmers about the problems they faced and offered helpful— and inexpensive—solutions. In addition, he was an excellent teacher who passed along practical knowledge as well as a love of nature to his students.

By the early 1920s, Carver was a national celebrity, hailed by both blacks and whites as the foremost black scientist of the day. He received many honors other than the Spingarn Medal, including the 1939 Roosevelt Medal for distinguished achievement in science. He was also named a Fellow of the Royal Academy of England. His last major project was to establish the George Washington Carver Museum and Foundation at Tuskegee. (Also see entry dated January 5, 1943.)

Garrett A. Morgan, a black inventor, developed the automatic traffic light. He later sold the patent to the General Electric Company for $40,000.

Morgan was born in Paris, Tennessee, in 1875. At the age of twenty, he moved to Cleveland, Ohio, where in 1901 he invented a belt fastener for sewing machines.

In 1914 Morgan won the First Grand Prize at the Second International Exposition of Sanitation and Safety for inventing a smoke inhalator. This inhalator was used in a successful rescue of workers trapped in a tunnel under Lake Erie in 1916. (The city of Cleveland later awarded Morgan a gold medal.) He also invented the gas mask American troops used during World War I.

Morgan died in 1963.

1924   **July 1.** Black tenor Roland Hayes was named a soloist with the Boston Symphony Orchestra. Earlier, he had received the Spingarn Medal for "so finely" interpreting the beauty of black folk songs. A native of Georgia, Hayes was born in 1887.

1925   **May 8.** A. Philip Randolph organized the Brotherhood of Sleeping Car Porters to work for fair employment practices for blacks employed by the railroads.

A. Philip Randolph in 1963

A pioneer in the black labor union movement, Randolph grew up in Florida. He was the son of a minister and a seamstress, both of whom were former slaves.

Randolph attended Cookman Institute in Florida and City College in New York. His scholarly interests as well as his practical experiences in Harlem left him with an intense hatred of racial bias and an enthusiasm for economic and social justice. He joined the Socialist Party and attempted to organize black students and workers. He also founded the socialist periodical the *Messenger,* which became one of the best magazines in the history of black journalism. During the 1930s, he served as president of the National Negro Congress.

In his later years, Randolph was an outspoken opponent of American intervention in foreign wars and segregation in the armed forces. In 1948, for example, he formed the League for Non-Violent Civil Disobedience Against Military Segregation and advised young black men to refuse to serve in the military until the government banned segregation and discrimination.

Randolph was also a consultant to several presidents on civil rights matters and was a key figure in both the 1941 and 1963 marches on Washington for jobs and freedom. (He called off the 1941 march at the last minute when President Franklin Roosevelt agreed to issue an order banning segregation and discrimination in the defense industry and government training programs.) Later, Randolph was one of two blacks named vice-presidents of the AFL-CIO, a new labor union created by the merger of the American Federation of Labor (AFL) and the Congress of Industrial Organizations (CIO).

Randolph died in 1979. (Also see entries dated June 25, 1941, and December 5, 1955.)

1926 **June 30.** The NAACP honored James Weldon Johnson with its Spingarn Medal for his careers as an executive secretary of the NAACP, a member of the U.S. Consul, editor, and poet.

Johnson was born in Florida in 1871 and went to school there. He continued his education at Atlanta University, New York's City College, and Columbia University. He began his professional life in Florida, working as a teacher, journalist, and lawyer before going to New York City to join his brother, J. Rosamond Johnson, as a writer of musical comedies.

Johnson is best known for his poetry and prose. His most famous works include *The Autobiography of an Ex-Colored Man* (1912), *The Book of American Negro Poetry* (1925), *God's Trombones* (1927), *Black Manhattan* (1930), a novel, and his own autobiography, *Along This Way* (1933). His poem "Lift Every Voice and Sing," which his brother set to music, became known as "the Negro National Anthem."

Johnson's social and professional contacts among blacks and whites in New York, along with his success as a writer and a diplomat and his "moderate" opposition to racial discrimination, made him the ideal choice as the NAACP's first executive secretary. In this position, Johnson led the campaign to outlaw lynching in the United States. His efforts resulted in the Dyer antilynching bill of 1921, which passed in the House of Representatives but failed in the Senate.

Before his death in 1938, Johnson taught for a while at Fisk University in Nashville, Tennessee. He has been called an "American Renaissance Man" in recognition of his many talents and interests.

1928 **November 6.** Oscar De Priest was elected to the U.S. House of Representatives from the state of Illinois. This made him the first black from a northern state to serve in Congress and the only black to do so since George H. White left in 1901.

The son of former slaves, De Priest was born in Alabama shortly after the Civil War.

He grew up in Kansas, where he worked as a painter. He then moved to Chicago and became involved in real estate and politics, serving as the city's first black alderman, or member of the city council. In 1928, he ran for and won a seat in Congress on the Republican ticket.

When De Priest first took office, he had a bad reputation among some blacks who thought he was corrupt and unwilling to fight for racial causes. By the end of three terms, however, he had proven himself to be an outspoken militant.

1929   **January 15.** Martin Luther King, Jr., regarded by many people as the greatest American of the twentieth century, was born in Atlanta, Georgia.

King's parents were members of the city's "black establishment." His father, Martin Luther King, Sr., was one of the city's leading black ministers. His mother, Alberta Williams King, was a teacher and the daughter of a prominent minister.

After finishing high school, King attended Atlanta's Morehouse College. At first, he did not plan to become a minister. But with the encouragement of Morehouse's president, Dr. Benjamin Mays, King decided he could find personal and professional satisfaction in the ministry. To that end, he continued his studies at Crozer Theological Seminary and Boston University.

In 1954, after completing the course work for his doctorate degree at Boston University, King returned to the South. He then became pastor of the Dexter Avenue Baptist Church in Montgomery, Alabama. It was there that King first made a name for himself as a leader in the civil rights movement when he helped organize the black community's famous bus boycott in 1955.

(Also see entries dated December 1, 1955; January 30, 1956; February 14, 1957; May 17, 1957; September 20, 1958; February 1, 1960; February 29-March 6, 1960; October 19, 1960; December 12-16, 1961; April 3, 1963; August 28, 1963; December 10, 1964; January 2-23, 1965; February 1-March 25, 1965; June 7-26, 1966; July 10-August 6, 1966; April 4, 1968; March 10, 1969; January 8, 1970; January 15, 1970; June 21, 1974; June 29, 1974; October 29, 1974; January 2-26, 1975; January 12-15, 1975; February 28, 1975; November 19, 1975; May 29-June 3, 1978; November 17, 1978; November 2, 1983; January 16, 1986; January 18, 1986; January 20, 1986; January 18, 1988; February 20, 1988; October 12, 1989; October 24, 1989; April 17, 1990; November 6, 1990; June 30, 1991; January, 1992; January 18, 1993; April 4, 1993; and May 6, 1993.)

October 29. The New York stock market crashed, marking the beginning of the Great Depression. During the Depression, blacks complained that they were "the last to be hired and the first to be fired."

Albon Holsey of the National Negro Business League organized the Colored Merchants Association in New York City.

Members of the organization planned to establish stores and buy their merchandise as a group. They then urged blacks to shop at these stores to help keep more blacks working. Within two years, however, the Depression had forced the stores out of business.

Meanwhile, the "Jobs-for-Negroes" movement got under way in St. Louis, Missouri, when the local chapter of the National Urban League (NUL) launched a boycott against a white chain store whose customers were almost all black but whose employees were almost all white. This movement spread to Chicago, Illinois, Cleveland, Ohio, New York City, Pittsburgh, Pennsyvania, and other major cities.

New York became the center of an especially intensive and sometimes bitter campaign. In 1933, the Citizens League for Fair Play began a drive to persuade white merchants to hire black sales clerks. Their motto was, "Don't Buy Where You Can't Work." As a result of this campaign, hundreds of blacks got jobs in Harlem stores and with public utility companies.

1930

March 31. President Herbert Hoover nominated North Carolina's Judge John J. Parker, a known racist, to the U.S. Supreme Court. The NAACP successfully blocked Parker's confirmation.

June 22. Educator, feminist, and civil rights spokesperson Mary McLeod Bethune was named one

Mary McLeod Bethune

of America's fifty leading women by the historian Ida Tarbell.

The child of former slaves, Bethune was born in Maysville, South Carolina, in 1875. After graduating from a Presbyterian Church mission school near her rural home, she studied at Scotia Seminary in North Carolina and at the Moody Bible Institute in Chicago, Illinois. She then taught for several years at various small schools throughout the South.

In 1904, Bethune heard about a major railroad construction project that was attracting thousands of unemployed black workers and their families to the east coast of Florida. Learning that conditions were especially bad near the resort town of Daytona Beach, she visited there herself and was very upset by the poverty and ignorance she encountered. Bethune immediately decided to establish a school for the black workers' children. She rented a rundown shack, fixed it up, and gathered (or made) whatever supplies she could. Later that same year, the Daytona Normal and Industrial School for Negro Girls opened its doors.

The school grew slowly but steadily, and in 1928 it merged with a nearby boys' school, the Cookman Institute, to become Bethune-Cookman College. Bethune served as its president until 1942.

During the 1930s, however, Bethune's other interests and activities kept her busy elsewhere, especially in Washington, D.C. In 1935, for example, she founded and headed the National Council of Negro Women. She was also a close advisor and friend to both President Franklin Roosevelt and his wife, Eleanor, and held several government posts in the late 1930s and early 1940s. (See entry dated December 8, 1936.)

In addition, Bethune was a popular speaker and contributed many articles to newspapers and magazines. She received the NAACP's Spingarn Medal in 1935 in recognition of her service to black education.

Bethune died in Daytona Beach on May 18, 1955.

1931   **April 6.** Nine black youths accused of raping two white women on a freight train went on trial for their lives in Scottsboro, Alabama. The case attracted international attention, with African American organizations, liberal whites, and the Communist Party all competing to defend "the Scottsboro Boys."

Despite shaky evidence, the defendants were quickly convicted. But the controversy dragged on for twenty more years, and by 1950 all nine men were free as a result of parole, appeal, or escape. (Also see entry dated October 25, 1976.)

August 4. Daniel Hale Williams, pioneer heart surgeon and founder of Provident Hospital, a predominately black institution in Chicago, Illinois, died in Chicago.

Williams was born in 1856 in Philadelphia, Pennsylvania, to a black woman and a white man. His father died when he was eleven, and his mother deserted him not long after that. For the next few years he supported himself by working on board a lake steamer and then as a barber.

Thanks to the generosity of a former surgeon on General Ulysses S. Grant's staff, Williams was eventually able to attend the Chicago Medical College. But he graduated at a time when black doctors were not allowed to practice in Chicago hospitals. So in 1891, he founded Provident Hospital and opened it to doctors and patients of all races.

It was at Provident in 1893 that Williams performed ground-breaking surgery on a man who had been stabbed in an artery very close to his heart. The man survived the delicate operation, but when Williams announced the news, many people doubted that a black doctor could have had anything to do with such an important event.

Squabbles among staff members at Provident eventually caused Williams to leave the hospital he had started. He then became the only black doctor on the staff of Chicago's St. Luke Hospital, and in 1913 he was named the first black member of the American College of Surgeons.

In addition to practicing medicine, Williams was an active member of the NAACP. He also promoted the building of hospitals and training schools for black doctors and nurses. Toward the end of his life, however, Williams was the target of harsh criticism from fellow blacks for leaving Provident and marrying a white woman. By the time of his death in 1931, he was a bitter and frustrated man.

1932   **November.** Franklin Roosevelt was elected president of the United States, promising a "New Deal" to everyone who was struggling to cope with the devastating effects of the Depression.

At about the same time, southern blacks began to leave the South in a new wave of migration that lasted until about the end of the 1930s. Faced with racial oppression and an economic crisis in farming, they headed to the major industrial centers of the North in search of jobs and more social freedom.

1933

March 15. The NAACP began its attack on segregation and discrimination in American schools and colleges when it sued the University of North Carolina on behalf of black applicant Thomas Hocutt. The NAACP lost the case, however, when a black educator who was supposed to certify Hocutt's academic record refused to do so.

1934

November 7. Arthur L. Mitchell, a Democrat, defeated Republican congressman Oscar De Priest of Chicago, Illinois to become the first black member of his party to serve in Congress.

Like De Priest, Mitchell was born in Alabama to former slaves. He received his education at Tuskegee Institute, where he was Booker T. Washington's office assistant, and at Talladega College in Alabama. Mitchell then taught school in rural Alabama and served as an assistant law clerk in Washington.

When he moved to Chicago, Mitchell was active in Republican politics at first. But like many other blacks, he switched to the Democratic party during the Depression years. Mitchell considered himself to be a "moderate," which did not make him a favorite of either the black press or the NAACP. He did, however, sponsor the long and costly suit that brought an end to segregation in railroad cars. (See entry dated April 28, 1941.) Mitchell served a total of four terms in Congress.

November. Elijah Muhammad became head of the Black Muslim movement in the United States.

Muhammad was born Elijah Poole in Sandersville, Georgia, in 1897. His father was a Baptist preacher, sawmill worker, and tenant farmer. As a young man, Elijah was deeply religious and very race conscious. He was working as a laborer in Georgia in 1923 when his white employer cursed him. Angered by the insult, Elijah decided to leave the South for what he hoped would be a better life up north. Settling in Detroit, Michigan, with his family, he worked at several different jobs until the Depression hit and the Pooles were forced to go on relief.

About this same time, Elijah came under the influence of W.D. Fard or Wallace Fard Muhammad, a mysterious black silk peddler. Fard had been telling blacks that they were members of a superior race that was descended from Muslims of Afro-Asia. Claiming to be a messenger from Allah, or God, he said he had been sent to reclaim his lost people and save them from the inferior race of "white devils" who had made their lives so miserable. Christianity, he insisted, was a false religion used by white people to keep blacks enslaved.

Elijah Muhammad

Elijah Poole soon became Fard's closest associate. When Fard mysteriously disappeared in 1934, Poole—known by then as Elijah Muhammad—took control of the group as "The Messenger of Allah to the Lost-Found Nation of Islam in the Wilderness of North America."

During World War II, Muhammad and his Black Muslim followers created an uproar when they refused to fight for the United States and sided with Japan instead. Muhammad himself was convicted of encouraging resistance to the draft and served time in a federal prison. He was released in 1946.

Meanwhile, Muslim membership dropped from a high of about 8,000 under Fard's leadership to 1,000. But during the 1950s and especially the 1960s, the Black Muslims saw their numbers increase. Even the bitter conflict between Muhammad and his most famous follower, Malcolm X, did not destroy the Nation of Islam. It has remained an important religious, political, and economic influence among urban blacks in particular. (Also see entries dated July 31, 1960; March 12, 1964; and February 25, 1975.)

1935   **June 25.** African Americans received an emotional boost when boxer Joe Louis defeated Primo Carnera, a white man, at Yankee Stadium in New York City. The six-round fight ended in a knockout and earned Louis the nickname "The Brown Bomber."

Born Joe Louis Barrow in 1914 in Lafayette, Alabama, the future heavyweight champion grew up in Detroit, Michigan. After leaving school, he worked in an automobile plant and boxed as a hobby in his spare time.

In 1934, Louis decided to turn professional. He was already well-known throughout the Midwest when he fought Carnera. Louis went on to defeat another former champion, Max Baer, and then was himself knocked out by German boxer Max Schmeling. But "The Brown Bomber" kept at it, beating several other challengers for the chance to face heavyweight champion Jim Braddock. On June 22, 1937, Louis defeated Braddock to become the new heavyweight champion of the world. Despite interrupting his career to serve in World War II, he held the title until 1949, longer than any other boxer.

A series of bad marriages and business ventures left Louis nearly penniless after his retirement from the ring. A comeback attempt in 1950 failed, and he quit boxing for good. (Also see entries dated June 22, 1938; April 12, 1981; and June 22, 1993.)

1936   **August 9.** African Americans cheered the news that Jesse Owens, a black track star, had won four gold medals at the Summer Olympics held in Berlin, Germany. Owens's first-place victories embarrassed German leader Adolf Hitler, who promoted the theory that Aryans, or people of German and Scandinavian descent, were racially superior to all other humans.

Owens was born in Ohio in 1913. He began competing in track and field at the Fairmount Junior High School in Cleveland and continued through his years at Ohio State University.

Jesse Owens

Owens was still a student at Ohio State when he won the 100-meter dash, the 200-meter dash, the long jump, and, with his three teammates, the 400-meter relay at the 1936 Olympics. These record-breaking triumphs led the Associated Press to name him the outstanding track athlete of the first 50 years of the 20th century.

Upon his return to the United States, however, Owens found that his gold medals meant nothing to potential employers. Discrimination made it difficult for him to earn a living until well into the 1950s. Eventually, he entered the field of public relations, heading his own company as well as acting as a spokesman for various charities, corporations, and the Olympics. (Also see entry dated March 31, 1980.)

December 8. President Franklin Roosevelt appointed Mary McLeod Bethune to his unofficial "Black Cabinet" as director of the Division of Negro Affairs of the National Youth Administration. (Also see entry dated June 22, 1930.)

1937 **March 26.** Black lawyer William H. Hastie was confirmed as the first African American federal judge. He had been chosen to serve in the District Court of the Virgin Islands, a U.S. possession southeast of Florida.

The son of a federal clerk, Hastie was born in Knoxville, Tennessee. He graduated with honors from Amherst College in 1925 and taught junior high school in New York before attending Harvard Law School.

Hastie entered government service during the early years of President Franklin Roosevelt's New Deal as an assistant solicitor, or lawyer, in the U.S. Department of the Interior. His historic nomination for a District Court judgeship was approved by the U.S. Senate despite strong opposition from some southerners. They considered him a "leftist," mostly because he supported civil rights activities. Among those who favored his nomination, however, were the NAACP (which later awarded him the Spingarn Medal) and influential whites at the Harvard Law School.

After completing his two-year term in the Virgin Islands, Hastie headed the Howard University Law School from 1939 until 1946. During part of this same period, he also served in President Franklin Roosevelt's "Black Cabinet" as a civilian aide to the secretary of war. He eventually resigned from this job in protest against the War Department's failure to act against segregation in the Air Force. (Also see entries dated May 1, 1946; October 15, 1949; and April 14, 1977.)

May 25. Artist Henry Ossawa Tanner died. Critics consider him to be the best of the early African American painters.

Born in 1859 in Pittsburgh, Pennsylvania, Tanner was raised in Philadelphia. At about the age of twelve, he was fascinated by the sight of a landscape painter at work in a local park. So he borrowed some money from his mother, bought some art supplies, and began to teach himself to paint. Going against the wishes of his father, an AME bishop, Tanner soon decided to become a painter rather than a minister. In 1880, he was accepted at the Pennsylvania Academy of Fine Arts. There he studied under Thomas Eakins, a famous artist known for his attention to detail, light, and shadow.

Racial prejudice and a desire to study abroad led Tanner to leave the United States for France in 1891. Except for a brief period around 1893 when he returned to Philadelphia to recover from typhoid fever, he spent most of the rest of his life in Paris.

Tanner first gained fame for his paintings of scenes from the everyday life of southern blacks. One of his best-known early works is *The Banjo Lesson,* which shows an old black man teaching a young black boy how to play the musical instrument. Later, Tanner turned to religious themes and produced paintings such as *Daniel in the Lion's Den* and *The Raising of Lazarus.* He enjoyed considerable success in his adopted country and won several important awards. He was also the first black elected to the National Academy of Design.

In 1969, thirty-two years after Tanner's death, the Frederick Douglass Institute and the National Collection of Fine Arts co-sponsored the first American exhibition of his work. The ninety-piece exhibit opened in Washington, D.C., at the National Collection of Fine Arts and then traveled to seven other museums. It was the first one-man show by a black artist to tour the country's major museums.

In 1991, the Philadelphia Museum of Art sponsored an exhibit that brought together more than 100 paintings, drawings, photographs, and mementos. Together, they provided visitors with a look back at Tanner's entire life and career.

July 2. The NAACP presented Walter F. White, a writer and civil rights leader, with the Spingarn Medal. As the NAACP's longtime executive secretary, he had led the organization during the years it experienced some of its greatest courtroom victories against racial segregation. He was also honored for his investigations of lynchings and his tireless lobbying for a federal antilynching law.

White was born in Atlanta, Georgia, in 1893 and went to school there and in New York. A blue-eyed and blond-haired black man, he could have easily passed for a white person. But after the 1906 Atlanta race riot, he totally identified himself with African Americans. His pale complexion enabled him (with no threat of danger) to investigate hate crimes against blacks in the South and later reveal who had committed them.

White died on March 21, 1955, in New York City.

1938   **June 22.** Americans were glued to their radios as black boxer Joe Louis, the so-called "Brown Bomber," knocked out German boxer Max Schmeling to retain the world heavyweight title.

Joe Louis

It was the second match between the two men (Louis had lost the first time), and it came at a time when Nazi leader Adolf Hitler was proclaiming that the German people were superior to all other racial and ethnic groups. But Louis battered Schmeling to the ground only two minutes into the first round of the fight. Many people regarded his victory as a symbolic triumph over Hitler's racist theories. (Also see entries dated June 25, 1935; April 12, 1981; and June 22, 1993.)

December 12. In the case of *Missouri ex rel Gaines,* supported by the NAACP, the U.S. Supreme Court declared that states must provide equal educational facilities for blacks, even if they are separate from those for whites. Lloyd Gaines, the man who originally filed the complaint that led to the trial, mysteriously disappeared following the Court's decision.

Marian Anderson

1939   **March.** The Daughters of the American Revolution (DAR), an organization of women descended from men who fought in the Revolutionary War, refused to allow black singer Marian Anderson to perform in their auditorium in Washington, D.C., on account of her race.

A native of Philadelphia, Pennsylvania, Anderson had a rich, deep voice that Italian conductor Arturo Toscanini described as the kind that appears once in a century. She was born in 1902, and even as a young girl she impressed other members of her church choir with her exceptional talent. At the age of nineteen, she began taking private lessons with Italian voice coach Giuseppe Boghetti. Four years later, Anderson beat 300 other singers in a national music competition for the chance to perform as a soloist with the New York Philharmonic Orchestra. Her appearance there was a success, and soon she was booked for additional concerts.

After spending the early 1930s in Europe studying music and languages and performing to enthusiastic audiences, Anderson returned to the United States. She then toured throughout the country, becoming more and more popular with each passing year. In 1936, President and Mrs. Roosevelt invited her to sing at the White House, making her the first black American singer ever to perform there.

Anderson had just completed yet another successful European tour when the DAR barred her from singing in Washington's Constitution Hall. An outraged Eleanor Roosevelt immediately resigned from the group in protest. The Secretary of Interior then made the Lincoln Memorial available for the Anderson concert, which drew an audience of 75,000 on Easter Sunday of 1939. Later that same year, Eleanor Roosevelt presented the singer with the NAACP's Spingarn Medal in recognition of her musical accomplishments. (Also see entries dated January 7, 1955, and April 8, 1993.)

October 11. The NAACP Legal Defense and Educational Fund was organized with the goal of waging an all-out war on discrimination. Charles H. Houston, a brilliant lawyer who received his education at Amherst and Harvard, led the effort to bring together some of the nation's best legal talents to fight against the kind of bias that was supported by law.

1940   **February.** Richard Wright published his novel *Native Son,* a deeply moving story of the effects of racial oppression on black Americans. This book, along with his novel *Black Boy* (published five years later), made Wright one of the most important and influential black writers of the twentieth century.

Wright was born in 1908 on a plantation near Natchez, Mississippi. His family moved from town to town a lot when he was young, so he often missed school. As a result, he was mostly self-educated. In Memphis, Tennessee, for example, he borrowed books from a "whites only" library by pretending that he had a note from a white patron who wanted him to check out a few titles.

In 1932, Wright's extensive readings as well as his own experiences with oppression led him to join the Communist party, which he hoped would help him understand the causes of social injustice. Disappointed by the narrow-mindedness of his fellow party members, he dropped out in 1944.

Six years later, as an employee of the federal government's Writers Project, he published his first book. Entitled *Uncle Tom's Children,* it was a collection of four long stories about racial oppression and violence in the South. Wright's work received much praise and won an award as the best work of fiction by a Writers Project author. His next book was *Native Son,* which was popular with readers and critics. In addition to becoming a bestseller, it was made into a

Richard Wright

successful Broadway play. Later, a film version starred the author himself in the lead role. Another bestseller followed in 1945—the mostly autobiographical *Black Boy.*

In 1947, Wright moved to Paris, France. He continued to write fiction and nonfiction there until his death on November 28, 1960.

March. Hattie McDaniel received an Academy Award for her performance in the supporting role of Mammy in *Gone with the Wind.* She was the first black ever to win an Oscar. In addition to appearing in *Gone with the Wind,* McDaniel was in such films as *The Little Colonel* and *Showboat.*

Benjamin O. Davis, Sr., pins a medal on his son

October 16. Benjamin O. Davis, Sr., was appointed brigadier general in the U.S. Army, making him the highest ranking black officer in the armed services.

Davis was born in Washington, D.C., in 1877 and studied at Howard University. He entered the Army as a first lieutenant in 1898 and fought with the 8th Infantry during the Spanish-American War. Prior to the Second World War, Davis served in the Philippines, Liberia, and the state of Wyoming. He also taught military science at Wilberforce University in Ohio and at Tuskegee Institute.

During World War II, Davis served in Europe as an advisor on problems of black servicemen. After the war, he remained overseas to help carry out President Harry S. Truman's orders to desegregate the armed forces. At the time he retired in 1948, Davis was an assistant to the inspector general in Washington, D.C.

Davis received many awards and decorations during his long career, including the Distinguished Service Medal, the Bronze Star, the Croix de Guerre with Palm, and an honorary doctorate from Atlanta University. He died on November 26, 1970. His son, Benjamin, Jr., also had a noteworthy military career in the U.S. Air Force. (See entry dated October 27, 1954, for information on Benjamin O. Davis, Jr.)

1941   **April 28.** The U.S. Supreme Court ruled in a case brought by black Congressman Arthur L. Mitchell that separate railroad car facilities must be *substantially* equal— that is, close to, but not exactly, equal.

June 25. President Franklin Roosevelt issued an executive order (a special proclamation that has the force of law) banning racial and religious discrimination in defense industries and government training programs.

He took this action not long after meeting with A. Philip Randolph, head of the Brotherhood of Sleeping Car Porters, and other black leaders. At the meeting, the president urged them to call off an upcoming March on Washington against employment discrimination and segregation in the national defense program.

Randolph refused to back down, however, and pledged that 100,000 blacks would demonstrate as scheduled on July 1. But after Roosevelt issued his order, Randolph canceled the March on Washington.

July 19. President Franklin Roosevelt established a Fair Employment Practices Committee to monitor discrimination against blacks in defense industries.

African Americans praised this action as well as the president's executive order of June 25. They considered both to be revolutionary developments in black history— perhaps *the* most revolutionary developments since Abraham Lincoln issued the Emancipation Proclamation. They were soon disappointed, however, when discrimination continued in spite of the committee. Politics, government "red tape," and opposition in the South prevented the group from reaching its goals.

August 6. The first in a series of serious racial disturbances involving white and black soldiers and civilians, occurred aboard a bus in North Carolina.

December 7. The Japanese attacked the U.S. naval base at Pearl Harbor in Hawaii, and President Franklin Roosevelt prepared to ask Congress for a declaration of war.

In the harbor on that fateful day was the battleship *Arizona*. When the Japanese bombs began to fall, Doris (Dorie) Miller, a twenty-two-year-old black messman (food server) on board the *Arizona,* acted quickly to move his captain from the bridge to a safer place. He then manned a machine gun and shot down four Japanese planes. The commander of the Pacific fleet, Admiral Chester W. Nimitz, later awarded the Navy Cross to Miller for his heroism. In 1943, the young sailor was listed as missing in action (and presumed dead) in the South Pacific.

Dorie Miller

The U.S. Army established a school for black pilots at Tuskegee, Alabama. Some African Americans were against having a segregated training program. But since there had never been a school for black pilots before, most seemed to consider the move a step forward.

While the pilots learned what they needed to know at Tuskegee, ground crews trained at Chanute Field in Illinois. By the end of the year, the 99th Pursuit Squadron was ready for action. About 600 black pilots received their wings during World War II.

1942   **June.** A group of blacks and whites organized the Congress of Racial Equality (CORE) in Chicago, Illinois. They committed themselves to direct, nonviolent action to fight discrimination.

Their first major effort was a sit-in at a Chicago restaurant. (In fact, CORE developed the sit-in technique for use in civil rights demonstrations.) From there, CORE spread to other cities across the country, and in June, 1943, the national group was established.

During the 1960s, CORE was at the forefront of the civil rights movement. Members organized countless sit-ins and marches and also sponsored the famous "Freedom Rides" throughout the South during the spring and summer of 1961. (Also see entry dated May 4, 1961.)

July 20. The Women's Army Auxiliary Corps (WAC) was formed. Black as well as white women were accepted for military service.

November 3. William L. Dawson was elected to the U.S. House of Representatives from Chicago, Illinois. A leader among black congressmen for some twenty years, he was known as a clever political strategist.

Dawson was the son of an Alabama barber. He received his education at Fisk University and at a Chicago law school. After serving in the First World War, Dawson opened a law practice in Chicago and became interested in local politics.

He began as a precinct worker and soon won favor with the Thompson Republican "machine," a term used to describe a well-organized group of people who work closely with a particular politician. He served five terms (1933-43) on the Chicago city council as a Republican before switching to the Democrats after Franklin Roosevelt became president.

During World War II, Dawson became an important member of the Kelly and Daley Democratic machines in Chicago. He served as "ward boss" in five city districts, precinct captain, committeeman, and vice-chairman of the Cook County (Illinois) Democrats.

On the national scene, Dawson was vice-chairman of the Democratic National Committee. He retired from politics in 1970 and died a year later.

1943   **January 5.** Scientist and inventor George Washington Carver died. He was buried on the grounds of Tuskegee Institute, where he had spent most of his career as the so-called "Wizard of Tuskegee." (Also see entry dated September 4, 1923.)

May 12-August 2. A series of serious race riots occurred across the nation, resulting in the deaths of approximately forty people.

U.S. troops were called out in Mobile, Alabama, and Detroit, Michigan, where the clashes threatened to interrupt defense production. Other disturbances took place in Beaumont, Texas, and in New York City's Harlem district.

1944   **April 3.** The U.S. Supreme Court ruled in the case of *Smith v. Allwright* that the white primary, which had kept blacks from voting in the South, was unconstitutional.

The decision paved the way for blacks to participate in southern politics for the first time since Reconstruction. Many states responded to the court's ruling by creating new restrictions outside the law to make it difficult for blacks to vote.

April 24. The United Negro College Fund (UNCF) was founded.

The UNCF's job was to coordinate the fund-raising efforts of the country's private all-black colleges and universities. Many of these schools were facing the possibility of having to close because they did not have enough money to stay open.

August 1. Adam Clayton Powell, Jr., was elected to the U.S. House of Representatives from Harlem, making him the first black congressman from the East.

One of the most colorful and controversial politicians of the twentieth century, Powell was born in 1908 in New Haven, Connecticut. Shortly after his birth, he and his family moved to Harlem, where his father made a name for himself as a minister and political leader.

After being expelled from City College of New York, Powell finished his education at Colgate University. He then became an outspoke minister, publisher, and civil rights activist. During the Depression, for example, he led a group of Harlem ministers in a series of demonstrations against major businesses in the area to force them to hire blacks. He also organized various social and welfare programs sponsored by his congregation at the Abyssinian Baptist Church.

Powell began his political career in 1941 as the first black member of the New York City Council. Then came his election to Congress as Harlem's representative. There he continued his fight against racial discrimination. He challenged the unwritten rules that barred him from entering certain dining rooms and other public places and furiously debated southern segregationists.

As chairman of the powerful House Committee on Education and Labor Committee from 1960 to 1967, Powell supervised the passage of nearly fifty pieces of important social legislation. Perhaps the most famous were the so-called Powell Amendments, which tried to block the use of federal funds to build segregated schools.

But during the late 1960s, Powell's flamboyant lifestyle made him the target of a congressional investigating committee. The committee looked into some personal

legal troubles he was having as well as the possible misuse of money that was supposed to pay for his staff and various travel-related expenses. Their findings led Powell's fellow members of Congress to take drastic action against him during the first few months of 1967. They stripped him of his chairmanship of the House Committee on Education and Labor, fined him, and eventually expelled him from Congress. In April of that same year, Powell was overwhelmingly voted back into office in a special election that was held to fill his seat. Congress refused to reinstate him, however, so he filed a lawsuit challenging the constitutionality of his expulsion.

Adam Clayton Powell, Jr. (center), in January, 1967

In January, 1969, after much debate, members of Congress voted to seat Powell once again. But they went ahead and fined him for misconduct. They also took away his status as a senior member of the House of Representatives, leaving him virtually powerless in a legislature where he had once enjoyed so much power. Despite a Supreme Court ruling in June, 1969, that said the original decision to expel him from Congress had been unconstitutional, Powell was nearing the end of his political career. In 1970, after being hospitalized for cancer, Powell lost a Democratic primary election to another black, Charles Rangel. (Also see entry dated April 4, 1972.)

December 13. Black women were allowed to enlist in the Women's Naval Corps (WAVES).

1945 **August 15.** The Japanese surrendered and World War II ended. More than 1,000,000 blacks served in the conflict.

September 18. A huge anti-integration protest took place in the schools of Gary, Indiana, when 1,000 white students walked out of classes. This massive demonstration, unlike any other at the time, set the stage for the school integration troubles of the next thirty years.

1946

May 1. Former federal judge William H. Hastie was confirmed as governor of the U.S. Virgin Islands. This made him the first African American to govern a U.S. state or territory since Reconstruction. (Also see entries dated March 26, 1937; October 15, 1949; and April 14, 1977.)

June 3. The U.S. Supreme Court, in the case of *Morgan v. Virginia,* banned segregation in bus travel between two or more states.

The case grew out of an incident involving a black woman named Irene Morgan. Morgan was arrested and fined ten dollars for refusing to move to the back of a bus running from Gloucester County, Virginia, to Baltimore, Maryland. She appealed her conviction, and the case went all the way to the Supreme Court. Despite the high court's ruling, life for most black travelers did not change very quickly. Buses in southern states continued to practice segregation.

August 10-September 29. Serious racial disturbances occurred in Athens, Alabama, and Philadelphia, Pennsylvania. Nearly 100 blacks were injured.

December 5. President Harry S. Truman appointed a national Committee on Civil Rights to investigate racial injustices and make recommendations.

1947

April 9. Leaders of the Congress of Racial Equality (CORE) sent a group of "Freedom Riders" into the South to test the U.S. Supreme Court's June 3, 1946, ban against segregation in bus travel that crossed state lines. The Freedom Riders were usually black and white college students, ministers, and other people who volunteered to challenge local laws that required blacks to sit in the back of the bus. They often faced attacks from mobs of angry whites, and law enforcement officials rarely stepped in to protect them.

Earlier, CORE had pioneered the sit-in technique at segregated restaurants. Their new "Freedom Rider" demonstrations gained national attention. (See also entry dated May 4, 1961.)

April 10. Jackie Robinson joined the Brooklyn Dodgers to become the first black baseball player in the major leagues.

Born in Cairo, Georgia, in 1919, Robinson grew up in Pasadena, California. He attended the University of California in Los Angeles (UCLA), where he starred in football, basketball, and tennis. Robinson left school in his junior year and briefly played professional football before joining the Army during World War II. (Unlike professional baseball teams, professional football teams had welcomed black players as early as the turn of the century. Recruiting stopped during the 1930s but picked up again around the mid-1940s.)

After the war, Robinson signed up with the Kansas City Monarchs in Negro League baseball in the hope that it would some day help him land the job he really wanted—that of a physical education teacher and coach. He turned out to be one of the best players on the team, and soon he caught the eye of a scout for the Brooklyn Dodgers of the National League.

At the time, major league baseball was open only to whites. But Branch Rickey, the

Jackie Robinson

Dodgers' general manager, had been secretly planning for several years to bring a black man into the majors. He decided Robinson had the talent as well as the toughness and self-discipline to take that historic first step.

In 1945, Rickey signed Robinson to a contract and sent him to play with the Montreal Royals, the Dodgers' top farm club. After spending the 1946 season with the Royals, Robinson was called up to play with the Dodgers themselves in the spring of 1947. His presence on the field created quite a stir. He was often the target of racial slurs and insults from opposing players, fans, and some reporters. He also received hate mail and death threats. But with the support and encouragement of the National League, some of his teammates and other players, and his wife, Rachel, Robinson made it through that first season and even won rookie of the year honors.

Over the next nine years, Robinson compiled an exceptional record as a hitter and base-stealer and led his team to six World Series appearances. He retired from the majors in 1956 with a .311 lifetime batting average, and in 1962 he became the first black player elected to the Baseball Hall of Fame.

After his retirement from the game, Robinson worked for a variety of businesses, including a restaurant chain, a bank, a construction firm, and a life insurance company. He was also active in civil rights causes. Robinson died October 24, 1972, at his home in Stamford, Connecticut.

June 27. Percy Julian, a distinguished black research chemist who developed new drugs to treat arthritis and other diseases, received the NAACP's Spingarn Medal.

Born in Montgomery, Alabama, in 1898, Julian was the son of a railway clerk. He graduated with honors from DePauw University and taught at several schools, including Howard University, before completing some advanced studies at Harvard University and the University of Vienna.

Julian then went to work as an industrial chemist in Chicago for the Glidden Company. He eventually established his own company, Julian Laboratories, and earned a reputation for manufacturing soya products, hormones, and medicine. He died in 1975.

September 1. Charles Spurgeon Johnson assumed the presidency of Fisk University, becoming the first black man to head the Nashville-based school.

Johnson was born in Bristol, Virginia, in 1893 and attended Virginia Union

University and the University of Chicago. From the very beginning of his career, he focused on studies of black life in America. From 1917 to 1919, for example, Johnson directed the division of research for the Chicago Urban League, and in 1920 he organized a similar department for the National Urban League. He also investigated black migration for the Carnegie Foundation in 1918 and served on the Chicago Committee on Race Relations from 1923 to 1929.

By the time he became president of Fisk University, Johnson had already made a name for himself as a writer and sociologist, or a person who studies society and social relationships between groups of people. His major published works include *Shadow of the Plantation* (1934), *The Collapse of Cotton Tenancy* (1934), *The Negro College Graduate* (1938), and *Growing up in the Black Belt* (1941). In addition, Johnson founded and edited the National Urban League's magazine, *Opportunity,* and sponsored literary contests for young black writers during the Harlem Renaissance. He died in 1956.

October 29. President Harry S. Truman's Committee on Civil Rights formally condemned racial injustice in the United States in its famous report entitled "To Secure These Rights." The biracial group also called for a positive program to eliminate segregation from American life.

1948   **June 9.** A modern breakthrough in southern politics occurred when a black man, Oliver W. Hill, was elected to the city council in Richmond, Virginia.

July 14. Several southern delegates walked out of the National Democratic Convention after the party adopted a strong civil rights platform (a word used to describe a group's set of beliefs and plans for action). South Carolinians and Mississippians were at the head of the movement that formed the "Dixiecrat" party in protest against the Democrats.

July 26. President Harry S. Truman issued an executive order that called for equality of treatment and opportunity for all Americans in the armed forces This order started the process of ending segregation and discrimination in the military.

September 13. The United Nations Security Council approved the selection of Professor Ralph J. Bunche, a noted black political scientist, to take charge of peace negotiations in war-torn Palestine.

Bunche was born in a Detroit, Michigan, ghetto in 1904 and was raised by his grandmother in Los Angeles, California, after his parents died. A brilliant student, he graduated at the top of his high school class and then went on to the University of California, where he studied international relations and was also an outstanding debater and athlete. After graduating with honors, he went on to attend Harvard University and earned a master's degree in government.

Bunche began his career as a teacher at Howard University, then returned to Harvard to obtain his doctorate degree. From 1938 to 1940, he worked for Swedish sociologist Gunnar Myrdal on his landmark study of race relations in the United States, *An American Dilemma.*

During World War II, Bunche served in the U.S. government and helped write the agreement that established the United Nations (UN). After the war, he went to work for the UN and quickly made a name for himself as one of its best negotiators.

Bunche's skills were put to the test in 1948 when he took on the especially tough assignment of bringing peace to the Middle East, where Arab nations and the new country of Israel (formerly Palestine) were at war. Facing danger and discouragement with good humor, intelligence, and optimism, he finally managed to get the two sides to agree to stop fighting.

In recognition of his efforts, Bunche received the 1950 Nobel Peace Prize, making him the first black ever to win that honor. Later, he won both the NAACP's Spingarn Medal and the U.S. government's highest civilian award, the Medal of Freedom.

Bunche continued his work with the UN throughout the 1950s and 1960s as under secretary general and directed peace keeping missions in several other parts of the world. At home, he was active in the civil rights movement. He was a faithful supporter of the NAACP, for example, and played a key role in the 1963 March on Washington and the 1965 Selma to Montgomery march led by Martin Luther King, Jr.

Bunche retired from the UN in 1971 due to poor health. He died six months later on December 9, 1971.

1949   **October 3.** The first black-owned radio station, WERD, went on the air in Atlanta, Georgia.

October 15. William H. Hastie, former federal judge and governor of the U.S. Virgin Islands, was appointed a judge of the U.S. Court of Appeals for the Third Circuit. (Also see entries dated March 26, 1937; May 1, 1946; and April 14, 1977.)

1950   **April 1.** Charles R. Drew, who was often called "the father of the blood bank," died in an automobile accident in Burlington, North Carolina.

Drew was born in Washington, D.C., in 1904, and starred in academics, football, and track at Amherst College. He then went to Canada to study medicine at McGill University. After receiving his degree in 1933, Drew returned to the United States and taught at Howard University.

In 1940, while studying the characteristics of blood plasma at Columbia University Medical School in New York City, Drew wrote a paper on how to preserve and store (or "bank") blood for use in emergencies. He soon became known as an expert in the subject, and during World War II he organized a blood-collection system for both the British and U.S. governments. He also served as director of the American Red Cross blood donor project until he resigned in 1941 in protest against its policy of segregating blood donations by race. In 1944, the NAACP awarded him the Spingarn Medal for the blood

Charles R. Drew

99

plasma research that had contributed so much to human welfare.

After the war, Drew taught at Howard University Medical School. At the time of his death, he was chief surgeon and chief of staff at Freedman's Hospital in Washington, D.C.

Contrary to popular myth, Drew did not bleed to death after his accident because he was refused treatment at a whites-only hospital. Several black doctors who were with him at the time always insisted that this story was not true. Black scholars who have studied the circumstances surrounding Drew's death have concluded that he died of his injuries despite receiving excellent care at a white hospital.

May 1. Gwendolyn Brooks was awarded the Pulitzer Prize for her poetry collection *Annie Allen,* making her the first black writer to receive the honor.

Brooks was born in Topeka, Kansas, in 1917, but she grew up in Chicago, Illinois, and has always considered it to be her hometown. Encouraged by her parents, she read a lot and began writing poems when she was very young. Brooks published her first piece when she was only thirteen, and after that she regularly contributed poetry to the Chicago *Defender,* a major black newspaper. After graduating from high school, she attended Wilson Junior College and earned a degree in English in 1936.

Gwendolyn Brooks around 1953

Throughout the late 1930s and early 1940s, Brooks gained more and more recognition for her poetry, first in the Chicago area and then around the Midwest. In 1945, she published her first collection of poems, *A Street in Bronzeville.* Its look at the everyday lives of ordinary black people greatly impressed the critics. She followed this success with *Annie Allen,* a sequence of poems that tell the story of a black woman's journey to adulthood.

Brooks's later works have included a novel, several books for children, and a number of poetry collections. She has also contributed regularly to various magazines.

In addition to her own writing, Brooks has actively encouraged other poets through teaching, sponsoring poetry competitions, and visiting schools, prisons, and other institutions. In 1968, she was named poet laureate, or official poet, of the state of Illinois. Brooks has also served as the first black woman poetry consultant to the Library of Congress, and in 1989 the National Endowment for the Arts gave her its lifetime achievement award.

June 27. The United States intervened in the Korean conflict. Thousands of blacks were among those fighting in the war.

1951

April 24. The University of North Carolina joined a growing list of major southern and border state universities that were beginning to admit black students.

May 24. The Municipal Appeals Court in Washington outlawed segregation in District of Columbia restaurants. Mary Church Terrell, the black feminist leader, was the leader of the local antisegregation movement. (Also see entry dated July 21, 1896.)

June 21. William H. Thompson of Brooklyn, New York, received the Congressional Medal of Honor posthumously (after his death) for heroism in Korea. It was the first such award to a black soldier since the Spanish-American War. Private Thompson died at his machine gun after refusing to withdraw in the face of overwhelming enemy forces.

July 12. Governor Adlai Stevenson of Illinois ordered the National Guard to stop a riot in Cicero, Illinois.

The disturbance began when more than 3,000 whites protested a black family's attempt to move into a home in an all-white neighborhood. Some observers called this riot the worst one in the North since 1919, when a series of racial disturbances erupted in cities across the country after World War I.

October 1. The U.S. Congress shut down the last all-black army unit, the 24th Infantry.

December 25. A new era of racist assassinations began with the bombing death of Florida NAACP leader Harry T. Moore in Mims, Florida.

1952

January 12. The University of Tennessee became the latest major southern university to admit black students.

December 7. The Southern Regional Council, an interracial civil rights group, announced that racist bombings were increasing in the nation. About forty had been reported since January, 1951.

December 30. The Tuskegee Institute announced that no lynchings occurred during 1952. It was the first time in the seventy-one years that the Institute had been keeping count of lynchings that none were reported.

1953

June 8. In the case of *District of Columbia v. John R. Thompson Co., Inc.,* the U.S. Supreme Court supported the decisions of lower courts that stated restaurants in Washington, D.C., could not refuse to serve well-behaved blacks. It upheld an 1873 law that made it a criminal act for owners of public eating places to refuse to serve any person just because of race or color.

June 19. Blacks protesting discriminatory treatment began a bus boycott in Baton Rouge, Louisiana.

August 4. Another serious riot erupted in Illinois to protest integrated housing. About 1,000 police officers were needed to quiet a disturbance that began at the Trumbull Park apartments in Chicago.

December 31. Hulan Jack, a native of the West Indies, became president of the Borough of Manhattan, New York. Before that time, no other black had held such a high post in city government.

1954   **March 4.** President Dwight Eisenhower named J. Ernest Wilkins Assistant Secretary of Labor, making him the top-ranking black person in the executive branch of the federal government.

May 17. In the landmark case of *Brown v. Board of Education of Topeka, Kansas,* the U.S. Supreme Court ruled unanimously that racial segregation in public schools was unconstitutional because separate educational facilities were by their very nature unequal.

The case took its name from a lawsuit filed on behalf of Linda Brown, a student in the Topeka, Kansas, public school system. Hers was actually just one of five separate but similar suits that the NAACP had filed to challenge racial segregation laws.

The Court's decision in the Brown case overruled *Plessy v. Ferguson,* the 1896 case that had established the idea of separate-but-equal public facilities. (See entry dated May 18, 1896.) Attorney Thurgood Marshall led the NAACP legal team that won the Brown case. It was their greatest victory in a series of favorable court rulings

Newspaper headline announcing the *Brown* decision

that occurred during the 1940s and 1950s.

September 7-8. Massive school desegregation began in the public schools of Washington, D.C., and Baltimore, Maryland. This was the first widespread school desegregation since the U.S. Supreme Court decision of May 17, 1954.

October 27. Benjamin O. Davis, Jr., the son of U.S. Army General Benjamin O. Davis, Sr., became the first black general in the U.S. Air Force.

Born in Washington, D.C., in 1912, the younger Davis attended Western Reserve University, the University of Chicago, and the U.S. Military Academy at West Point. In 1936, he became only the fourth black man to graduate from West Point.

Davis trained at the Tuskegee Advanced Flying School in 1942 and became commander of the 99th Fighter Squadron at the air field there. Ordered to North Africa in 1943, at the height of World War II, he led the 15th Air Force bombers in their important attacks on Romanian oil fields. Later, he saw action in Italy.

Since World War II, Davis has served in Korea (where he was commander of the 51st Fighter-Interceptor Wing during the Korean conflict), Japan, Taiwan, Germany, and at several bases on the U.S. mainland. He has received many awards and decorations, including the Distinguished Service Medal, the Silver Star, the Legion of Merit, and the Distinguished Flying Cross. (See entry dated October 16, 1940, for information on Benjamin O. Davis, Sr.)

October 30. Desegregation of the U.S. armed forces ended when the Defense Department announced it had abolished all-black units.

November 2. Charles C. Diggs, Jr., was elected to the U.S. House of Representatives. The thirty-three-year-old Diggs was the first black congressman from Michigan. He joined fellow black congressmen William Dawson of Chicago (who had been reelected to his seventh term in 1954) and Adam Clayton Powell, Jr., of Harlem (who had won his sixth term in 1954).

Diggs's election marked the first time in the twentieth century that as many as three blacks served in Congress. All were Democrats.

1955   **January 7.** Black contralto Marian Anderson fulfilled a lifelong dream when she became the first black to sing with New York City's Metropolitan Opera. She made her debut as Ulrica in a production of Giuseppe Verdi's *A Masked Ball*. (Also see entries dated March, 1939, and April 8, 1993.)

April 11. Roy Wilkins became the third executive secretary of the NAACP following the death of Walter White on March 21.

Wilkins was born in 1901 in St. Louis, Missouri, but grew up in St. Paul, Minnesota, in the home of an aunt and uncle. After graduating from high school, he attended the University of Minnesota and was editor of the student newspaper. Racial violence he witnessed during his college years led him to join the NAACP so that he could work actively against discrimination.

In 1923, Wilkins became managing editor of the *Kansas City Call*. It was in that

Roy Wilkins

Missouri town that he came to realize how deeply rooted the system of segregation could be. So he made up his mind to devote his career to fighting for equal justice.

In 1931, Wilkins joined the staff of the NAACP, taking a leading role as the organization's assistant executive secretary. In 1943, for example, he represented the interests of blacks in the Philadelphia, Pennaylvania, transit strike, and following the *Brown v. Board of Education of Topeka, Kansas* decision in 1954, he supervised the NAACP's efforts to make school desegregation a reality. He also served as editor of the NAACP's magazine, *Crisis,* from 1934 until around 1949.

After becoming the organization's executive secretary, Wilkins quickly distinguished himself as an outstanding speaker and writer on behalf of the civil rights movement. He quietly but effectively led the NAACP throughout the 1960s and most of the 1970s and continued to attack discrimination through the courts.

Toward the end of his career, Wilkins was the target of criticism from younger and more militant black leaders who thought he was not radical enough. But eventually he was recognized by all as a man whose accomplishments ranked him as one of the major figures of the civil rights era along with such men as Martin Luther King, Jr., Malcolm X, Whitney Young, and A. Philip Randolph. (Also see entry dated September 8, 1981.)

May 21. Rock musician and composer Chuck Berry recorded "Maybellene," which reached number one on the R&B charts by mid-September. Over the next six years, he followed it with ten more hits, including "Roll Over Beethoven," "Rock and Roll Music," "Sweet Little Sixteen," and "Johnny B. Goode."

Born on October 18, 1926, Berry learned how to play guitar when he was a teenager. But he ran into trouble with the law and spent time in reform school during the 1940s. He then worked on an automobile assembly line before making it big as a rock star.

Berry influenced an entire generation with his guitar playing and showmanship, which included his famous "duckwalk." In fact, David Marsh of *Rolling Stone* magazine claims that "Chuck Berry is to rock what Louis Armstrong was to jazz."

Among the many honors he has received during his long career are a 1984 Grammy Award for Lifetime Achievement and a 1987 Lifetime Achievement Award from *Guitar Player* magazine. In 1986, Berry was elected to the

Chuck Berry

Rock and Roll Hall of Fame. Despite his ongoing problems with the law, he still performs occasionally.

May 31. Citing the *Brown* decision of May 17, 1954, the U.S. Supreme Court ordered the nation's school systems to desegregate "with all deliberate speed." The vagueness of this phrase allowed school segregation to continue across the nation for several more decades.

Rosa Parks being fingerprinted after her arrest

August 28. Lynchings were renewed in the South with the brutal slaying of a fourteen-year-old Chicago youth, Emmett Till, in Money, Mississippi. Till had been accused of making indecent advances toward a white woman.

November 25. The Interstate Commerce Commission (ICC) banned segregation in public vehicles (such as trains and buses) that traveled across state lines. The order also extended to waiting rooms in stations.

December 1. Rosa Parks, a black seamstress in Montgomery, Alabama, defied the order of a local bus driver and refused to give up her seat to a white person and move to the back of the bus. She was then arrested for violating "Jim Crow" segregation laws. The black community responded with a city-wide bus boycott that began on December 5.

Despite terrorist attacks (including the bombing of the homes of boycott leaders), legal harassment, massive arrests, and civil suits, the boycott continued until December 13, 1956, when the U.S. Supreme Court ruled that segregation on public buses in Montgomery was illegal. Another significant result of the boycott movement was the emergence of Martin Luther King, Jr., as a national civil rights leader.

Parks herself eventually moved to Detroit, Michigan, with her family to escape the threats and persecution that followed her courageous decision. There she went to work in the office of U.S. Representative John Conyers. Nowadays, Parks spends a great deal of her time speaking to and helping young people.

December 5. Two black labor leaders, A. Philip Randolph and Willard S. Townsend, were elected vice presidents of the AFL-CIO.

December. Rock musician and singer Little Richard's "Tutti Frutti" was released just before Christmas and reached number twenty-one on the charts by the end of the month.

Born in December, 1932, in Macon, Georgia, Richard Penniman was one of twelve children raised by devout Seventh Day Adventist parents. According to Little Richard himself, they forced him to leave home at the age of thirteen because he was gay. He then moved in with a white family while performing at their Macon nightclub.

The gospel singing and piano training Little Richard had received in church gave him an early edge in the music business. By 1951 he had cut his first recordings, which included "Every Hour," "Why Did You Leave Me?," and "Get Rich Quick." After the success of "Tutti Frutti," he had a string of hits, among them "Long Tall Sally," "Slippin' and Slidin'," "Lucille," and "Good Golly Miss Molly."

But in the late 1950s, Little Richard gave up rock and roll to devote himself to Bible study at a Seventh Day Adventist seminary. He eventually received a bachelor's degree from Oakwood College in Huntsville, Alabama, and was ordained a minister. By the mid-1960s, however, he was touring once again, this time in England with the Beatles, who were then on the verge of international stardom.

Performing old—and, with less success, new—songs, Little Richard has continued to attract fans of all races with his energized piano-playing and campy look. He has made numerous television appearances, and in 1986 he had a major role in the movie *Down and Out in Beverly Hills.*

1956   **January 30.** The home of Martin Luther King, Jr., was bombed in Montgomery, Alabama.

February 3. The desegregation of major Southern universities continued with the court-ordered admission of a black coed, Authurine Lucy, to the University of Alabama. But school officials suspended Lucy after a February 7 anti-black riot on campus and expelled her on February 29 for making "false" and "outrageous" statements about them.

June 30. Mordecai Johnson retired as president of Howard University.

Born in Paris, Tennessee in 1890, Johnson was educated at Morehouse College, the University of Chicago, Rochester Theological Seminary, and Harvard University. In 1923, upon receiving his master's degree in sacred theology from Harvard, he attracted national attention for a speech he gave entitled "The Faith of the American Negro."

After teaching at Morehouse and Howard, Johnson became Howard's first black president in 1926. The school he took over at that time was not very well respected in the academic community, so Johnson worked hard to improve Howard's standing. In 1928, he persuaded Congress to pass an act that would set aside money for the school on a yearly basis to help support and develop various programs.

By the time he retired, Howard University was a success that boasted an enrollment of more than 6,000 students, some of whom were white. It had ten separate schools and colleges, including a School of Medicine that was producing about half of the black doctors in the United States. It was also fully accredited, meaning that the instruction it offered met certain standards of quality.

August 30-September 17. Anti-black protests and violence erupted when efforts began to desegregate schools in Mansfield, Texas; Clinton, Tennessee; and Sturgis and Clay, Kentucky.

November 13. The U.S. Supreme Court upheld the decision of a lower court outlawing segregation on buses in Montgomery, Alabama.

Martin Luther King, Jr. (center row), and Ralph Abernathy (front row) mark the end of the Montgomery bus boycott

December 20-21. The Montgomery bus boycott ended when public buses in the Alabama city were desegregated.

December 25-26. The home of black clergyman and civil rights activist Fred L. Shuttlesworth was bombed in Birmingham, Alabama. The city's blacks responded by defying bus segregation laws. At least forty people were arrested.

December 27. After blacks boycotted the buses of Tallahassee, Florida, for more than six months, segregation on board the vehicles was finally outlawed.

1957

February 14. The Southern Christian Leadership Conference (SCLC) was organized in New Orleans, Louisiana. The city of Atlanta, Georgia, became the group's national headquarters, and Martin Luther King, Jr., was elected its first president.

May 17. More than 15,000 Americans, mostly black, gathered at the Lincoln Memorial in Washington, D.C., to demonstrate support for a voting rights act. Martin Luther King, Jr., led the speakers with shouts of "Give us the ballot!" It was the first large-scale black protest in Washington since the end of World War II.

June. Blacks in Tuskegee, Alabama, began boycotting local white merchants to protest the actions of the state legislature.

White Alabama politicians had angered blacks by "gerrymandering," or redividing the voting districts of Tuskegee in such a way that the black districts were smaller. This unfair tactic made it more difficult for blacks to gain political power.

July. In England, African American tennis star Althea Gibson became the first black woman to win the women's singles title at the famed Wimbledon tournament.

Gibson was born in South Carolina in 1927 but grew up in the Harlem district of New York City. She was a tough and undisciplined youngster who often skipped school to hang out in the street or go to the movies. But as a teenager she displayed a talent for paddleball (a form of tennis) that caught the eye of a city recreation department worker named Buddy Walker. Thinking that Gibson might do well at regular tennis, Walker bought her a racket and arranged for her to play against professional Fred Johnson at an interracial New York club. Johnson was equally impressed, as were other club members who saw that the teenager's skills were definitely above average. They paid for her to take lessons from Johnson, who taught her the basics of the game and helped her improve her overall technique.

Within a year after she had begun working at tennis, Gibson was on her way to success. She won the girls' singles title in the New York State Open Championship in 1942 and again in 1944 and 1945. She began playing on the women's circuit in 1946, and even though she failed in her attempt to win the singles title, she attracted the attention of Hubert Eaton and Robert W. Johnson. These two black doctors had made a second career out of helping promising young black tennis players, and they felt Gibson had a great deal of potential. So they both saw to it that she received further training and that she finished high school and went on to college.

Gibson was a standout performer in women's tennis for the next ten years, from the late 1940s through the late 1950s. Because tennis had always been a game of well-to-do white people, she broke down many barriers in the process as the first black to play in major lawn tennis tournaments. In 1950, for example, she was the first black to compete at prestigious Forest Hills on New York's Long Island. After that, many other clubs in the United States and overseas opened their courts to her, too.

In 1957, Gibson became the first black woman to play and win at Forest Hills and Wimbledon in singles and doubles competition. She triumphed again at both championships in 1958, then retired from tennis at a time when she was ranked as the best female player in the world.

Since then, she has tried her hand at many things, including professional golf and public relations work. More recently, Gibson has been involved in planning women's and girls' sports activities for private clubs and government-run programs in New Jersey.

August 29. The U.S. Congress passed the Voting Rights Act of 1957, the first major civil rights legislation since 1875.

September 9. Violence aimed at preventing school desegregation continued in the South. A school in Nashville, Tennessee, was bombed and the clergyman Fred L. Shuttlesworth was attacked in Birmingham, Alabama, while trying to enroll his children in school.

September 24-25. After unsuccessfully trying to persuade Arkansas governor Orval Faubus to give up his efforts to block desegregation of Central High School in Little Rock, President Dwight Eisenhower ordered federal troops into the city to stop people from interfering with federal court orders.

The Little Rock incident was the most serious clash between a state government and the federal government in modern times. Faubus and a mob of whites backed down in the face of military power and finally allowed nine black children to begin attending a desegregated high school on September 25.

August 19. Members of the NAACP Youth Council began a new series of sit-ins, this time at segregated lunch counters in Oklahoma City, Oklahoma.

Troops escort black students at a newly integrated school

September 20. Martin Luther King, Jr., was stabbed and seriously wounded by a crazed black woman while in Harlem autographing copies of his story of the Montgomery bus boycott, *Stride toward Freedom.*

1959   **March 11.** Lorraine Hansberry's play *A Raisin in the Sun* opened on Broadway. The story of a black family's frustrating efforts to move out of the ghetto and into a white neighborhood, it was the first play by a black woman to appear on the New York stage. (It was also produced, directed, and acted by blacks.) Later that year, Hansberry became the first black to win the New York Drama Critics Circle Award for the best play of 1959.

A native of Chicago, Illinois, Hansberry was born in 1930. After graduating from high school, she briefly studied art at the Chicago Art Institute, the University of Wisconsin, and in Mexico. It was while she was still at the University of Wisconsin that she walked in on a play rehearsal one day and was so fascinated by what she saw that she decided to try to do some writing for the stage.

Not long after, Hansberry headed for New York City. There she went to work as a reporter for Paul Robeson's radical black newspaper, *Freedom.* Hansberry remained with the paper until 1953, when she was able to quit her job and devote most of her time to her own writing.

A Raisin in the Sun was Hansberry's very first play, and it was an instant success with critics and audiences, black as well as white. (An equally popular movie version starring Sidney Poitier followed in 1961, and in 1974 a Broadway musical adaptation entitled *Raisin* won a Tony Award.) Hansberry's second Broadway play, *The Sign in Sidney Brustein's Window,* opened shortly before its author died of cancer on January 12, 1965.

April 25. Another Mississippi lynching was recorded with the death of Mack Parker of Poplarville.

1960   **February 1.** A wave of sit-ins at segregated lunch counters, led mostly by black college students, began at Greensboro, North Carolina. Four students from North Carolina A&T College started the new movement. In less than two weeks it had spread to fifteen cities in five southern states, and within two years it had flooded the South.

113

Angry whites responded to the sit-ins with physical violence and legal harassment, including massive jailings. But most restaurants eventually desegregated as a result of court orders or new laws.

The success of the sit-in technique encouraged blacks to use this method of nonviolent direct action in other areas where discrimination was still common. Martin Luther King, Jr., stepped forward to lead the expanded movement.

A lunch counter sit-in

February 25-27. On February 25, black students from Alabama State University conducted a sit-in demonstration at the County Courthouse in Montgomery. This was the first protest of this type in the capital of the former Confederacy. The local sheriff and his deputies kept close watch on the demonstrators in the courthouse lunchroom while groups of white men, some armed with baseball bats, patrolled outside.

On February 27, a white man with a club struck a black woman on the head and injured her, but the police made no arrests. Two days later, Alabama governor John

Patterson warned that there were not enough police officers in the country to prevent disturbances and offer protection if blacks continued "to provoke whites."

February 27. Black and white demonstrators were attacked in Nashville, Tennessee, in two of the five stores where students had staged nonviolent lunch counter sit-ins. Police arrested about 100 people, mostly black demonstrators. To protest the injustice of this treatment, about three-quarters of them chose to go to jail rather than pay a fine or post bond while they waited for their cases to go to trial.

February 29-March 6. On February 29, Martin Luther King, Jr., spoke to a crowd of more than 1,000 students at Alabama State University in Montgomery, Alabama, following three days of racial tensions caused by student sit-ins.

King urged the students to continue fighting segregation with passive resistance, a protest technique that involves refusing to cooperate with authorities without becoming violent. The students pledged to withdraw from the university as a group if any of them were expelled for participating in a sit-in.

On March 1, blacks marched to the old Confederate capitol building in Montgomery, where they prayed and sang the "Star-Spangled Banner" during a nonviolent protest against segregation. The next day, the State Board of Education expelled nine of the Alabama State University students who attended the demonstration.

On March 6, state, county, and local police stopped a march of nearly 1,000 blacks on their way to a protest meeting at the Alabama state capitol. There were scattered fistfights between blacks and a mob of jeering whites, but police prevented large-scale violence.

Two days later, Montgomery police broke up another protest demonstration on the campus of Alabama State University and arrested thirty-five students and at least one teacher. Thirty-three of the blacks were later found guilty of disorderly conduct and fined $200 each.

March 4. Lunch counter sit-ins reached the southwest part of the country when about 100 students from Texas Southern University held nonviolent protests in Houston. Three days later, in an apparent act of revenge, four masked white men kidnapped a black man, beat him, and then carved the letters KKK on his chest and stomach.

April 15-17. The Student Nonviolent Coordinating Committee (SNCC) was founded in Raleigh, North Carolina. A civil rights organization made up mostly of black and white college students, SNCC arranged sit-in activities across the nation and helped thousands of blacks register to vote.

April 19. In Nashville, Tennessee, the home of black city councilman and NAACP attorney Z. Alexander Looby was destroyed by a dynamite bomb. Looby and his family escaped injury, but the bomb damaged several other homes in the neighborhood. It also blew out hundreds of windows at the nearby Meharry Medical College (a black school), where several students were injured by flying glass.

Looby had served as the attorney for more than 100 college students arrested in Nashville sit-ins since demonstrations had begun in February, 1960. After the bombing, more than 2,000 blacks marched on the Nashville City Hall protesting the police's failure to stop the racial violence.

May 6. President Dwight Eisenhower signed into law the Voting Rights Act of 1960. It was supposed to strengthen the Voting Rights Act of 1957, which had given additional protection to blacks who wanted to vote. Under the new law, federal courts could appoint "voting referees" who would have the power to register blacks in areas where there was a proven history of racial discrimination against voters.

July 31. Elijah Muhammad, leader of the Black Muslims, called for the establishment of an all-black state.

The idea of creating such a state (or group of states) later became a symbol and rallying cry for new supporters of black nationalism, a movement that favors separate political, social, economic, and cultural actions and institutions for black people.

September 7. In Rome, Italy, black track star Wilma Rudolph became the first American woman to win three gold medals in the Olympics.

Wilma Rudolph

A native of Tennessee, Rudolph was born in 1940, the twentieth of twenty-two children. A bout with polio when she was only four years old partially paralyzed her left leg and foot. But through a combination of her mother's massage therapy and young Wilma's own determination to get rid of the leg brace and special shoe she had to wear, she was able to overcome her handicap by the time she was twelve.

Once she was free to run and play like other children, Rudolph threw herself into sports. At first, she specialized in basketball and was a star player on her high school team. Then she switched to track and showed so much potential that she was offered a scholarship to Tennessee State University. There Rudolph joined the women's track team, known as the Tigerbelles. She quickly made a name for herself as the fastest Tigerbelle and easily qualified for the 1960 Olympic team after completing her second year of college.

Rudolph earned her three gold medals by winning the 100-meter dash, the 200-meter dash (in record time), and the 400-meter relay. It was the best an American woman had done in track since 1932, the year Babe Didrikson won two gold medals. But more important to Rudolph personally was the fact that she had won as many medals as her idol, Jesse Owens, the star of the 1936 Olympics. (See entry dated August 9, 1936.)

Rudolph's triumphs—as well as her warm and friendly personality—made her a media celebrity in Europe and as well as in the United States. Within a year or so after the Olympics, she was showered with a number of prestigious honors. The Associated Press named her the Woman Athlete of the Year, for example, and in 1962, she won the Babe Didrikson Zaharias Award as the most outstanding female athlete in the world.

Rudolph retired from competition in 1962. Since then, she has worked in a variety of teaching and coaching positions in schools and for community programs. She has also promoted women's health and fitness and served as a special consultant on minority affairs at Indiana's DePauw University. In 1981, she established the Wilma Rudolph Foundation to help young athletes train for national and international competition while helping them plan for a life and career after they give up sports.

October 19. Martin Luther King, Jr., and approximately fifty other blacks were arrested for sitting-in at an Atlanta, Georgia, department store restaurant. A judge in Decatur, Georgia, then revoked King's parole for a previous conviction on a minor traffic violation and sentenced him to serve four months in Georgia's maximum security prison. Robert F. Kennedy and his brother, John F. Kennedy (who was then a presidential candidate), helped King's family obtain his release.

November 10. President-elect John F. Kennedy named Andrew Hatcher associate press secretary. Hatcher was for a time the highest-ranking black appointee in the executive branch of the federal government.

November 14. Desegregation crept into the major industrial centers of the South when black children were admitted to schools in New Orleans, Louisiana.

On November 10, U.S. District Judge J. Skelley Wright had stopped the state from putting new anti-school-integration laws into effect. That same day, the New Orleans school board approved plans to admit five black children to two previously all-white schools.

On November 13, the state legislature took control of New Orleans schools, fired the school superintendent, and ordered all schools closed on November 14. Judge Wright then issued a new order banning the state from interfering with the schools.

As angry white parents jeered at them, four black children enrolled in the two schools on November 14. White protests, including a boycott, continued for most of the rest of the school year.

1961   **January 11.** A riot led to the suspension of two black students at the University of Georgia. Neither had been attending the school for very long when they were forced to leave. They were readmitted following a court order on January 16.

January 27. Singer Leontyne Price made her first appearance with New York's Metropolitan Opera in *Il Trovatore*. The audience cheered her performance with an unheard-of forty-two-minute standing ovation, and soon she was on her way to becoming one of the world's leading sopranos and the first black singer to gain international stardom in opera.

Price was born in Laurel, Mississippi, on February 10, 1927. At the age of nine, she attended a concert by African American singer Marian Anderson and decided then and there to devote her own life to music.

After graduating from Wilberforce College in 1949, Price attended the Juilliard School of Music in New York and studied voice with former concert singer Florence Page Kimball. While at Juilliard, she sang in student productions, performed in a Broadway show, and starred in a revival of George Gershwin's *Porgy and Bess.*

Leontyne Price

Price gave her first solo concert at New York's Town Hall in 1954. The following year, she became the first black singer to perform opera on television.

In 1957, Price was invited to fill in for another singer in the lead role of Verdi's *Aida*. Her interpretation of the part was so stunning that she and her perfect "Verdi voice" are considered the standard against which all other *Aida* performances should be judged.

Although she is closely identified with *Aida,* Price appeared in more than 100 other Metropolitan Opera productions during her long career. She also sang throughout the United

States and Europe. Her many recordings have brought her additional fame, including thirteen Grammy Awards.

Among the many other awards Price has received are the Presidential Medal of Freedom (the nation's highest civilian award) in 1965, the Kennedy Center Honors for lifetime achievement in the arts in 1980, and the first National Medal of the Arts in 1985. In 1978, she was invited to perform at the White House, and in 1982, she opened the convention of the Daughters of the American Revolution (DAR) at Washington's Constitution Hall with a concert honoring her childhood idol, Marian Anderson. The DAR had once barred Anderson from singing in the very same hall on account of her race. (See entry dated March, 1939.)

Since retiring from the Metropolitan Opera in 1985, Price has devoted most of her time to solo concerts, teaching, and writing.

February 11. Robert C. Weaver, a black housing expert with a doctorate degree from Harvard University, became administrator of the Housing and Home Finance Agency. It was the highest federal post ever held by an African American up to that time.

May 4. A group of white and black youths, sponsored by the Congress of Racial Equality (CORE), set out on a bus trip through the South to test desegregation practices. The biracial group had to put up with physical violence (including savage beatings), arson, and legal harassment to prove that despite court rulings and orders from the Interstate Commerce Commission (ICC), many southern states still discriminated against black travelers.

In the fall, the ICC once again ordered an end to discrimination in transportation. While it eventually disappeared on the vehicles themselves, it continued in waiting rooms and other facilities, especially in the rural South.

August 9. President John F. Kennedy named fifty-year-old Chicago attorney James B. Parsons judge of the District Court of Northern Illinois. It was the first such position for an African American in the continental United States. Parsons was a judge on the Cook County Court at the time of his appointment. (Also see entry dated June 19, 1993.)

September 1. In Atlanta, Georgia, ten black children peacefully integrated four high schools. President John F. Kennedy praised residents of the Deep South's largest city and expressed the hope that school desegregation was entering a new, nonviolent stage.

September 23. President John F. Kennedy named NAACP chief counsel Thurgood Marshall judge of the Second Circuit Court of Appeals, which included the states of New York, Connecticut, and Vermont.

Marshall was fifty-three at the time of his appointment and had been with the NAACP for more than twenty years. Southern segregationists in Congress did everything they could to stall his confirmation, but finally—after nearly a year of controversy—the Senate voted to approve Marshall for the judgeship. (Also see entries dated July 13, 1965; June 13, 1967; June 27, 1991; and January 24, 1993.)

December 12-16. Martin Luther King, Jr., and his supporters launched an all-out attack against segregation and discrimination in Albany, Georgia.

Mass arrests and political tricks eventually caused their efforts to fail. But it taught civil rights leaders valuable lessons that they remembered when planning future direct-action assaults on segregation by large groups of demonstrators.

1962

January 18-28. Officials at Louisiana's Southern University, the largest all-black state college in the South, closed the school after students began protesting the expulsion of sit-in demonstrators.

Under pressure from state authorities, administrators at many publicly supported black colleges used expulsions and shut-downs to stop sit-ins and related activities. Later in the 1960s and 1970s, this became a common way of dealing with student disturbances.

May 17. Sociologist and historian E. Franklin Frazier died in Washington, D.C. Frazier was the author of the controversial book *Black Bourgeoisie,* which argued that the black middle class was isolating itself from the problems of poverty-stricken blacks.

Born in Baltimore on September 24, 1894, Frazier graduated from Howard

University in 1916 and received his doctorate degree from the University of Chicago in 1931. He returned to Howard in 1934 and spent the next twenty-five years there as chairman of the sociology department. He also taught for brief periods at other schools, including Columbia University and New York University.

In 1948, Frazier was named president of the American Sociological Society. Later, he served as chairman of UNESCO's committee of experts on race and as chief of UNESCO's Applied Science Division in Paris, France.

Recognized as an authority on the black family, among other subjects, Frazier wrote numerous books. Besides *Black Bourgeoisie,* they included *The Negro Family in the United States, The Negro in the United States, The Negro Church in America, The Free Negro Family and Race,* and *Culture Contacts in the Modern World.*

August. President John F. Kennedy named Marjorie Lawson an associate judge in the District of Columbia Juvenile Court. She was the first black woman appointed to a judgeship by a president of the United States.

A native of Pittsburgh, Pennsylvania, Lawson was born in 1912. She earned a degree in social work from the University of Michigan, then went on to Terrell Law School in Washington, D.C. She later received a second law degree from Columbia University.

For many years, Lawson combined a private law practice (in partnership with her husband) with government and civic service aimed at improving conditions in the black community. She also wrote a weekly newspaper column for about fourteen years during the 1950s and 1960s.

A friend and supporter of John F. Kennedy, Lawson was active in both his 1956 and 1960 tries for the Democratic presidential nomination. After his election in 1960, Kennedy turned to her when he approved the expansion of the juvenile court system in the District of Columbia. She held a judgeship there until 1965, when she resigned to devote more time to local politics and community affairs.

September 9. Two black churches were burned in Sasser, Georgia. Burnings and bombings of black churches, especially those used for civil rights meetings, were common during the 1960s.

September 30. U.S. Supreme Court Justice Hugo Black ordered the University of Mississippi to admit black student James H. Meredith. The governor of Mississippi, Ross Barnett, tried unsuccessfully to stop the young man from attending "Ole Miss."

On the day that U.S. marshals escorted Meredith to class, a riot erupted on the campus in Oxford, Mississippi. National Guard troops eventually restored order. Meredith graduated from the university in 1963.

1963   **April 3.** Martin Luther King, Jr., led civil rights forces in a drive against discrimination in Birmingham, Alabama.

The city's police force, headed by Commissioner Eugene "Bull" Connor, used dogs and high-powered water hoses against demonstrators. This brutality and the mass arrests that followed aroused public opinion, especially in the North. President John F. Kennedy hoped the violence would help him win support for the civil rights proposals he had presented to Congress on March 1.

The Birmingham protests continued until May 10, when city officials signed an agreement calling for gradual desegregation of public accommodations. This touched off a series of bombings at the homes and businesses of black leaders, which in turn led to hours of black rioting.

June 11. Although Governor George C. Wallace tried to block their entrance, two black students were finally admitted to the University of Alabama. President John F. Kennedy had ordered National Guard troops to make sure officials allowed the blacks to enroll.

In a television address that evening, Kennedy called for an end to discrimination through changes in the laws as well as in the hearts and minds of all Americans. Despite the president's impassioned plea, Congress still did not take any action on his civil rights proposals.

June 12. Medgar W. Evers, NAACP field secretary in Mississippi and a World War II hero, was gunned down by a sniper in Jackson, making him the latest victim of assassination resulting from civil rights activity. The man accused of the crime, a white segregationist named Byron de la Beckwith, was eventually acquitted when a jury could not reach a verdict in the case. (Also see entry dated December 16, 1992.)

June-August. Civil rights demonstrations, protests, and boycotts occurred in almost every major urban area in the country.

In June, for example, blacks in Boston, Massachusetts, and Harlem, New York, protested for an end to discrimination in the construction industry and segregation in the schools. In July, officials in Cambridge, Massachusetts, declared limited martial law after black demonstrators and white segregationists clashed.

August 27. Scholar, activist, and NAACP co-founder W.E.B. Du Bois died in Ghana, Africa, at the age of ninety-five. He had moved to Africa in 1961 after losing all hope that black Americans would ever know freedom in their native land. (Also see entries dated 1903; July 11-13, 1905; February 12, 1909; 1910; and February 19-21, 1919.)

August 28. The largest single protest demonstration in U.S. history occurred at the Lincoln Memorial in Washington, D.C., where 250,000 blacks and whites gathered to demand that Congress pass sweeping civil rights legislation.

Martin Luther King, Jr., thrilled the crowd with his immortal "I Have a Dream" speech. President John F. Kennedy met with a group of civil rights leaders at the White House and promised to keep pushing for antidiscrimination laws.

September 15. Racial tensions flared up again in Birmingham, Alabama, when four young black girls died in the bombing of the Sixteenth Street Baptist Church. No serious disturbances followed the incident.

October 22. A massive boycott involving nearly 250,000 students took place in Chicago, Illinois, to protest school segregation.

November 22. Black Americans joined the world in mourning the death of President John F. Kennedy at the hands of an assassin. Many of them believed he had been killed because he supported civil rights. Congress was still debating the president's proposed legislation at the time of his death.

Martin Luther King, Jr., at the 1963 March on Washington

1964   **January 21.** President Lyndon B. Johnson named black journalist Carl T. Rowan director of the U.S. Information Agency (USIA). It was the first of several appointments President Johnson made that put blacks into high-ranking government positions.

January 23. The U.S. Congress adopted the 24th Amendment to the Constitution. This new amendment declared that no one could be denied the right to vote just because he or she did not pay a "poll tax" or any other kind of tax. Officials in several southern states had long used a "poll tax" to discourage or disqualify black voters who could not afford to pay the special tax.

February. In an upset victory, boxer Muhammad Ali knocked out Sonny Liston to win the world heavyweight championship.

Under his birth name, Cassius Clay, Ali had won the 1960 Olympic gold medal as a light heavyweight and then turned professional. In 1963, he became a Black Muslim and changed his name.

A flamboyant master of self-promotion, Ali made a name for himself with his words as well as his fists. He proclaimed himself to be "the greatest" and declared of his boxing style, "I float like a butterfly and sting like a bee."

March 12. Black Muslim minister Malcolm X announced he was dropping out of Elijah Muhammad's Nation of Islam to establish his own movement.

Muhammad Ali

A persuasive speaker with a fiery tongue, Malcolm X was born Malcolm Little in Omaha, Nebraska, in 1925. His father, Earl Little, was a Baptist minister and an outspoken supporter of Marcus Garvey's "Back to Africa" movement in the early 1900s.

In 1931, when Malcolm was only six, his father was found dead on some streetcar tracks not far from the family's home in Lansing, Michigan. The police called it an accident, but the Littles believed he had been murdered by whites who opposed his support of black nationalism. In any case, Earl Little's death shattered the family. In 1937, his wife was committed to a state mental hospital after a series of emotional breakdowns, and his eight children were placed in foster homes.

Malcolm grew into a troubled teenager who dropped out of school and turned to a life of crime, including gambling, drug-dealing, and burglary. He was serving time in a Massachusetts prison during the 1940s when he first came upon the teachings of Elijah Muhammad and the Black Muslims. (See entry dated November, 1934.) By the time he was released from jail in 1952, he was an enthusiastic believer in Islam. (It was around this time that he also decided to take the surname "X" in place of the "slave name" Little.)

Making his way to the Nation of Islam's headquarters, he met with Elijah Muhammad himself and impressed the older man with his intelligence and forceful personality. Within just a few months, Malcolm X was named a minister and given a position at a Detroit mosque. He studied for a while under Elijah Muhammad and then was given the responsibility of starting several new Muslim congregations across the country. In 1957, he founded the movement's newspaper, *Muhammad Speaks,* and by 1959 he had become one of the leading spokesmen for the Black Muslims.

The message Malcolm X shared with his audiences was not what they were used to hearing from such "mainstream" leaders as Martin Luther King, Jr., who supported nonviolent integration. Instead, Malcolm X called for black separatism and encouraged his followers to take up arms in self-defense against white hatred. His fiercely militant views alarmed many blacks and most whites, who feared his words would lead to a race war.

As Malcolm X's personal appeal and media exposure brought him a larger following, Elijah Muhammad reportedly began to consider him ambitious and dangerous. In November, 1963, Malcolm X publicly referred to the assassination of President John F. Kennedy as an example of "chickens coming home to roost." Elijah Muhammad immediately suspended Malcolm X and paved the way for him to leave the movement a few months later.

Malcolm X then made a pilgrimage to Mecca, the holy city of Islam, and traveled across the Middle East and Africa. He returned to the United States a changed man. Having taken on a new name—El Hajj Malik El-Shabazz—he began to soften his views on black separatism and white racism.

But the tensions between Malcolm X and Elijah Muhammad continued throughout the rest of 1964 and into 1965. Malcolm X was very critical of the Nation of Islam, accusing the group of misusing funds and making suspicious contacts with white supremacist organizations. He also denounced Elijah Muhammad as a fake, a racist, and an immoral man who had fathered at least eight children by several young Muslim women. As Malcolm X worked to establish two new groups of his own—Muslim Mosque, Inc., and the Organization of Afro-American Unity—he became the target of death threats that he thought came from the Black Muslims. (Also see entries dated February 14, 1965; February 21, 1965; and November 18, 1992.)

Malcolm X

April 13. Sidney Poitier became the first black actor to win an Academy Award for Best Actor. He was honored for his role in the movie *Lilies of the Field.*

July 2. After overcoming southern-sponsored attempts to stall action on the bill, the U.S. Congress passed the historic Civil Rights Act of 1964. It was the most important legislation of its kind since 1875. Among its many features was a ban on discrimination in public accommodations and in employment.

July 18-August 30. Serious racial disturbances occurred in a number of American cities, leaving more than 100 people injured and causing millions of dollars in property losses.

The first one erupted in the Harlem section of New York City after white police officers shot a black teenager. Riots also took place in Brooklyn and Rochester, New York; Jersey City, New Jersey; Chicago, Illinois; and Philadelphia, Pennsylvania. Clashes between blacks and white police officers were to blame for some of these riots, too. In many cases, officials had to call out National Guard troops to stop the violence.

August 4. The bodies of three young civil rights workers, James E. Cheney, who was black, and Michael Schwerner and Andrew Goodman, who were white, were discovered in a shallow grave on a farm outside of Philadelphia, Mississippi.

The FBI accused nearly twenty white segregationists—including several law enforcement officers—of being involved in the murders. But the federal charges against the suspects were dropped later in the year. In 1967, however, three white men from Meridian, Mississippi, were convicted on conspiracy charges in the deaths and eventually sentenced to three years in federal prison. They were released in 1972 after serving slightly more than two years of their sentences.

December 10. Martin Luther King, Jr., the champion of non-violent resistance to racial op-

Martin Luther King, Jr. (left), and his wife, Coretta, meet with Ralph Bunche at U.N. headquarters

pression, was awarded the Nobel Peace Prize in Oslo, Norway. Only thirty-five years old, he was the youngest man in history and the second African American to receive this prestigious honor. United Nations official Ralph Bunche was the first, in 1950.

December. The U.S. Congress passed the Economic Opportunity Act as part of President Lyndon Johnson's "War on Poverty."

This legislation later was the target of severe criticism for its inefficiency, even from people who had originally supported it. Nevertheless, it created many programs that have been helpful to blacks, including Head Start for pre-schoolers, Upward Bound for high school students, and college work-study financial aid.

1965   **January 2-23.** Civil rights forces led by Martin Luther King, Jr., opened a voter registration drive in Selma, Alabama.

King was attacked as he registered at a formerly all-white Selma hotel, but he was not seriously injured. On January 19, local law enforcement officers began arresting would-be black voters and their supporters. On January 23, however, a federal district court issued an order prohibiting anyone from interfering with people seeking the right to vote.

February 1-March 25. The drive to register black voters in Alabama grew into a nationwide protest movement after whites in and around Selma stiffened their resistance and civil rights leaders intensified their efforts.

On February 1, law enforcement officers arrested more than 700 blacks, including Martin Luther King, Jr. On February 26, a black demonstrator, Jimmie L. Jackson, died from wounds he received at the hands of state troopers in Marion, Alabama. On March 7, several hundred protestors in Selma faced billy clubs, tear gas, whips, and cattle prods as they attempted to march across a bridge. On March 11, three white businessmen attacked James Reeb, a white minister from Boston, Massachusetts, who had been helping in the voting rights drive. He later died from the assault, but his accused attackers were found not guilty of murder.

From March 21-25, protesters staged a fifty-mile "Freedom March" from Selma to the Alabama state capitol at Montgomery to dramatize their cause. (Federal troops protected them from possible violence after a federal judge ordered state officials

Martin Luther King, Jr., leads supporters on the Selma-to-Montgomery March

not to interfere with the march.) On March 25, as many as 50,000 people gathered in front of the capitol building to hear Martin Luther King, Jr., and others criticize Alabama leaders for interfering with voting rights. The crowd then presented Governor George Wallace with a petition.

Later that same night, Viola Gregg Liuzzo, a white civil rights worker from Michigan, was murdered. Four members of the Ku Klux Klan were arrested and charged in connection with her death. Only three of them were eventually convicted of conspiracy to violate Liuzzo's civil rights.

February 14. In New York City, unknown attackers firebombed the home of Malcolm X. He and his family escaped without injury. (Also see entries dated March 12, 1964, and February 21, 1965.)

February 21. While preparing to speak to a group of his followers at Harlem's

Audubon Ballroom, Malcolm X was assassinated by three men who had ties to the Black Muslims.

Just a few weeks before his death, Malcolm X had finished his autobiography, which was published later in 1965. A joint project with *Roots* author Alex Haley, *The Autobiography of Malcolm X* has become a classic of twentieth-century black American literature. Its message of black unity, pride, and self-reliance still has tremendous appeal, especially among many younger blacks who have begun to look to Malcolm X as a symbol of strong leadership. (Also see entries dated March 12, 1964; February 14, 1965; and November 18, 1992.)

May 26. The U.S. Congress passed a new voting rights bill, the Voting Rights Act of 1965.

This new law prevented states from denying the right to vote to people who could not or would not pay a special poll tax. It also granted the right to vote to people who were unable to read or write English but who could demonstrate that they had an eighth-grade education in a school conducted under the American flag. In addition, the Voting Rights Act of 1965 stated that if local officials refused to register eligible voters, federal officials could register them instead.

June 10-16. Blacks in Chicago, Illinois, staged another round of demonstrations against the slow pace of school desegregation in their city. The target of their frustration was a superintendent they viewed as segregationist. When he was given a new one-year contract, a coalition of civil rights groups decided to hold a public school boycott in protest.

Despite orders from a federal judge blocking the boycott, the demonstrations began on June 10. The very next day, 225 people were arrested, including entertainer Dick Gregory, Congress of Racial Equality (CORE) director James Farmer, and nine clergymen. The protests continued until Chicago mayor Richard Daley approved a downtown march and agreed to negotiate with civil rights leaders.

July 13. President Lyndon Johnson named Appeals Court Judge Thurgood Marshall solicitor general of the United States. This was the highest law enforcement position ever held by an African American. As solicitor general, Marshall acted as the government's chief legal spokesman in cases that appeared before the

Fires burn in Watts

U.S. Supreme Court. (Also see entries dated May 17, 1954; September 23, 1961; June 13, 1967; June 27, 1991; and January 24, 1993.)

August 11-21. The Watts section of Los Angeles, California, was the scene of a devastating race riot—the most serious disturbance of its kind that America had ever seen.

As was the case in several other cities that had been rocked by riots a year earlier, a clash between blacks and white police officers started the trouble. National Guard troops helped stop the disorder. By then, 34 people had died and almost another 900 had been injured. More than 3,500 people were arrested, and property losses reached nearly $225 million.

Afterwards, federal, state, and local authorities began looking at ways to improve living conditions in the twenty-square-mile ghetto of 100,000 people. On August 20, President Lyndon Johnson condemned the Watts rioters and refused to accept "legitimate grievances" as an excuse.

September 15. Comedian Bill Cosby became the first black actor to star in a television series with the debut of "I Spy." He and co-star Robert Culp were secret agents who traveled around the world on assignment. Culp posed as a top tennis player and Cosby pretended to be his trainer.

1966

January 3. Floyd McKissick, a militant black civil rights leader from North Carolina, succeeded James Farmer as director of the Congress of Racial Equality (CORE).

McKissick was born in Asheville, North Carolina, in 1922. His long career as a civil rights activist began after he had trouble entering the all-white University of North Carolina Law School. With the help of Thurgood Marshall, who was then a lawyer for the NAACP, McKissick fought his way into the school under a federal appeals court order.

After receiving his degree and serving in World War II, McKissick opened a practice in Durham, North Carolina. There he handled a number of civil rights cases, including one involving his own daughter's attempt to enroll in a previously all-white public school.

Before becoming director of CORE, McKissick served as the group's national chairman for three years. Under his leadership, CORE changed from an interracial organization that supported nonviolent integration to an aggressive, mostly black group dedicated to black political and economic liberation—even if it led to separatism.

Floyd McKissick speaks at a CORE rally in 1967

January 10. By a vote of 184-12, members of the Georgia House of Representatives denied newly elected Julian Bond his seat in the state legislature for opposing U.S. involvement in the Vietnam War.

Bond had told journalists on January 6 that he supported the SNCC's call for an alternative to the military draft that might involve social service or civil rights work instead. Many white Georgia legislators thought his statements reflected an "un-American attitude." The seven other black members of the House voted to support Bond. (Also see entry dated January 8, 1967.)

January 13. President Lyndon Johnson named Robert C. Weaver the first secretary of the new Department of Housing and Urban Development (HUD). This made him the first African American to serve in a presidential cabinet in U.S. history and the highest-ranking black in the executive branch of the government.

One of the nation's leading authorities on urban housing, Weaver had enjoyed a long and successful career in government. He had previously served as housing director for New York and as a member of President Franklin Roosevelt's "Black Cabinet." He had also been the highest-ranking black in President John F. Kennedy's administration.

January 25. President Lyndon Johnson named former NAACP attorney Constance Baker Motley judge of the U.S. District Court for Southern New York. She was the first African American woman to hold a federal judgeship.

Motley was born in Connecticut in 1921 to parents who had come to the United States from the Caribbean island of Nevis. She briefly attended Fisk University before transferring to New York University, where she earned an economics degree in 1943. Three years later, she received her law degree from Columbia University.

Motley then went to work full-time for Thurgood Marshall at the NAACP Legal Defense and Educational Fund. (She had been working there part-time while she was still in school.) She spent some twenty years there, serving as associate counsel during a period when the civil rights movement won most of its important legal victories against segregation.

In 1964 Motley entered politics, first as a member of the New York State Senate (the first black woman to hold that office) and then as president of the Borough of Manhattan (once again as the first black woman to hold that office). Her achievements in civil rights soon began to attract national attention, and in 1966 President Johnson made his historic appointment. Motley became the chief judge of her court in 1982, remaining in that position until she retired from the federal bench in 1986.

Constance Baker Motley with President Lyndon Johnson

Stokely Carmichael at left and H. Rap Brown of the SNCC

May 16. Black political activist Stokely Carmichael became head of the Student Non-Violent Coordinating Committee (SNCC).

Born in 1941 in Trinidad, Carmichael came to the United States when he was eleven and grew up in a New York City ghetto. A good student who was offered scholarships to a number of white universities, he chose to go to Howard instead. There he joined CORE's student sit-in movement. After graduating from college in 1964, he became a member of SNCC and rose to the leadership position just two years later.

A handsome and energetic young man with a flair for the spoken word, Carmichael quickly changed SNCC into a more militant organization that had racial liberation as its goal. Later, he left SNCC for the even more revolutionary Black Panthers. He soon resigned, however, when he disagreed with the group's efforts to join forces with white radicals. In 1969, Carmichael moved to Guinea, changed his name to Kwame Toure and began working for the Pan-African movement.

June 6. James H. Meredith, the first black student to attend the University of Mississippi in 1962, was shot but not seriously wounded during his one-man "March against Fear" from Memphis, Tennessee, to Jackson, Mississippi. Police arrested a white segregationist for the attack.

June 7-26. James Meredith's "March against Fear" resumed with civil rights activists such as Martin Luther King, Jr., and Stokely Carmichael in the lead. The demonstration ended with a rally of 15,000 people at the state capitol in Jackson, Mississippi. King, Carmichael, Meredith, and others spoke to the crowd.

It was during this march and rally that Carmichael and others began to use the phrase "Black Power." Although it meant different things to different people, "Black Power" showed that some blacks were ready to take a more aggressive stand on issues of importance to African Americans. CORE approved the "Black Power" concept at its national convention in July, but the SCLC and the NAACP avoided it.

July 10-August 6. Martin Luther King, Jr., spoke to a mostly black crowd of 45,000 in Chicago, Illinois, and launched a drive to get rid of segregation in the nation's third largest city.

Two days later, a riot broke out in one of Chicago's black ghettoes. It began after an argument between police and some black children who had opened a fire hydrant so they could play in the water. Two blacks were killed, many were injured, and 370 were arrested.

On July 15, King and Chicago mayor Richard Daley announced new recreation programs for Chicago blacks, a committee to study police-citizen relations, and closer cooperation between community residents and police. On August 5, however, King was leading another protest against discrimination in the city when white onlookers began throwing rocks at him. He was not seriously hurt, but he soon left Chicago. His antidiscrimination campaign had been only partially successful.

July 18-23. A serious racial disturbance occurred in Cleveland, Ohio after an incident in a neighborhood bar.

There were two versions of what had started the trouble. One version was that the bar's white management had refused to serve water to blacks. The second version was that the bar's management had thrown out a woman who was asking for donations to pay for a friend's funeral. Afterwards, groups of blacks began roaming around the neighborhood, and there were some shootings, bombings, and instances of looting.

Four people died in the riots and fifty others were injured. There were 160 arrests and widespread property damage, including at least ten buildings that were destroyed by fire.

October. Black revolutionaries Huey Newton and Bobby Seale established the Black Panther Party in Oakland, California.

Newton, who was born in Louisiana, and Seale, a native of Texas, both grew up in California. They met in 1960 while attending Merritt Junior College in Oakland. There they shared an admiration for the teachings of Malcolm X and a hatred for police brutality and other forms of white racism. At first, Newton and Seale were very active in the college's African American student association. Later, they dropped out of the group and organized the Black Panther Party instead.

The Black Panther Party adopted a ten-point program that outlined their demands for improvements in the areas of employment, education, and housing. They also called for the release of all black political prisoners, the trial of blacks only by black juries, an end to police brutality, and exemption from military service.

The Panthers insisted on "power to the people" and supported the idea of black self-defense, especially against hostile police. They favored a socialistic economy, a system in which the government (rather than private companies) owns and controls the production and distribution of goods. To help spread their ideas, the Panthers published their own newspaper. They also earned respect for providing food and educational programs to children.

Young blacks in the ghettoes of the North and of the West Coast especially admired the Panthers. But as their numbers and influence increased, so did their clashes with

Bobby Seale (left) and Huey Newton

law enforcement officers. (Also see entries dated September 8, 1968; August 19, 1969; December 4-5, 1969; August 29-31, 1970; August 31, 1970; August, 1970; September 5-7, 1970; October 19, 1970; May 25, 1971; August 8, 1971; December 15, 1971; November 2, 1974; and August 22, 1989.)

October. Thirty-two-year-old National Basketball Association (NBA) star Bill Russell was named player-coach of the Boston Celtics, making him the first black to head a major professional sports team.

One of the finest defensive players in NBA history, Russell was a four-time winner of the league's Most Valuable Player (MVP) award. He had led the Celtics to nine championships (eight of them in a row) before becoming the team's coach.

November 8. Edward W. Brooke, the attorney general of the state of Massachusetts, was elected U.S. senator from Massachusetts. A liberal Republican, Brooke was the first African American to sit in the U.S. Senate since Reconstruction.

Brooke was born in Washington, D.C., on October 26, 1919. His father was a lawyer with the Veterans Administration, and as a result, the Brooke family enjoyed a comfortable, upper-middle-class lifestyle.

After graduating from high school, Brooke entered Howard University with the idea of becoming a doctor. But he soon found that he did not enjoy his pre-med courses as much as he did subjects such as literature, history, political science, economics, art, and drama. He earned his bachelor's degree from Howard in 1941 and then served in the Army during World War II. After the war, he enrolled in Boston University Law School and received degrees from there in 1948 and 1949.

Brooke then set up a private law practice in suburban Boston. He first entered politics in 1950, when he ran for state representative and lost. A second try in 1952 also failed, and Brooke decided to drop out of politics while he worked to establish his law practice.

In 1960, Brooke reentered Massachusetts politics as a candidate for secretary of state. Although he lost the election by a narrow margin, he attracted the attention of other Republicans as an up-and-coming politician. In 1961, the state's new Republican governor named Brooke head of the Boston Finance Commission. There he made news for exposing corruption in various city departments.

A year later, Brooke ran for the office of attorney general. This time, his campaign

State police and National Guardsmen arrest looters in Newark, New Jersey

ended in success. It also made history, because he was the first black to be elected, except during reconstruction, to such a high office in the United States. At the time, he was also the highest-ranking black government official in all of the New England states.

Brooke served two terms as attorney general in Massachusetts before deciding to run for the U.S. Senate. His victory in the 1966 elections launched a twelve-year career that ended when Brooke returned to practicing law in 1979.

1967   **January 8.** Following a U.S. Supreme Court ruling, Julian Bond was finally able to take his seat in the Georgia state legislature. (Also see entry dated January 10, 1966.)

May 1-October 1. The United States experienced the worst summer of racial disturbances in the country's history as more than forty riots broke out and at least 100 other incidents occurred.

Smoke from numerous fires fill the skies above Detroit, Michigan

The most serious outbreaks were in Newark, New Jersey (July 12-17), where twenty-six people died, and in Detroit, Michigan (July 23-30), where forty people died. Trouble also surfaced in New York City; Cleveland, Ohio; Washington, D.C.; Chicago, Illinois; Atlanta, Georgia; and other cities.

Later that summer, President Lyndon Johnson assembled a National Advisory Commission on Civil Disorders to look into the disturbances and make recommendations. Commonly known as the Kerner Commission after its leader, Illinois governor Otto Kerner, it held a series of hearings and investigations and released a report during the spring of 1968. (Also see entry dated March 2, 1968.)

May 12. H. Rap Brown became the new chairman of the Student Non-Violent Coordinating Committee (SNCC). A militant supporter of black power, he went on to have numerous brushes with the law.

Brown disappeared in 1970 while awaiting trial on a charge of inciting a 1968 riot in Cambridge, Massachusetts. He surfaced again in October, 1971, when he was shot, arrested, and later convicted for holding up a bar in New York City. In 1972, Brown received an additional sentence from a U.S. district court judge in New Orleans, Louisiana, for his conviction on a 1968 federal weapons charge.

While in prison, Brown converted to Islam and changed his name to Jamil Abdullah Al-Amin. After his release, he moved to Atlanta, Georgia. He now runs a health food grocery store there and serves as a spiritual leader in his community.

June 13. President Lyndon Johnson nominated Thurgood Marshall to be an associate justice of the U.S. Supreme Court, recommending him to be the first African American to serve in that position.

Thurgood Marshall

A native of Baltimore, Maryland, Marshall was born in 1908. He attended Lincoln University (near Philadelphia, Pennsylvania) and then went on to the Howard University Law School, from which he graduated with honors in 1933.

As a young attorney in private practice, Marshall specialized in civil rights and criminal law. He also used his skills on behalf of the Baltimore chapter of the NAACP and soon attracted the attention of leaders of the national group in New York City. In 1936, they persuaded him to join their staff, and in 1940 he became director of the NAACP's newly formed Legal Defense and Education Fund.

Over the next twenty years, Marshall led the organization's fight in the courts against racial segregation in all areas of American life—voting, going to school, serving on juries and in the military, using sleeping and dining cars on trains, and buying and renting a place to live. He had many important victories among the cases he argued before the U.S. Supreme Court, including the historic *Brown v. Board of Education of Topeka, Kansas* in 1954. (See entry dated May 17, 1954.)

In 1961, President John F. Kennedy nominated Marshall for a federal judgeship. (See entry dated September 23, 1961.) In 1965, President Johnson named him solicitor general, a position in which he was responsible for arguing cases on behalf of the government before the U.S. Supreme Court. (See entry dated July 13, 1965.) Two years later came the nomination to the Supreme Court itself. Southern segregationists reacted just as they had back in 1961, when Marshall was first nominated for a federal judgeship. They delayed the confirmation process, attacking Marshall as an "activist" who was too "liberal." But on August 30, 1967, the Senate approved him as the new associate justice.

In the beginning, Marshall was a rather moderate voice among the five or six justices considered liberal. But as presidents Nixon, Ford, Reagan, and Bush replaced retiring liberal justices with conservatives throughout the 1970s and 1980s, Marshall increasingly stood alone as the only liberal voice on the court. Still, he continued to insist that the rights of the individual were more important than the rights of the state. He also battled all forms of discrimination and tried to educate his fellow justices about the effects of racism on American society. (Also see entries dated June 27, 1991, and January 24, 1993.)

John Coltrane

July 17. Saxophonist John Coltrane, whose music played a major role in the development of modern jazz, died of liver cancer just months after cutting his final album, *Expression.*

Coltrane was born on September 23, 1926, in North Carolina. During the 1940s, he played with several different groups, including a U.S. Navy band. Late in the decade, he joined Dizzy Gillespie's orchestra. He stayed with Gillespie for four years and experimented even then with technical innovations and compositions.

During the 1950s, Coltrane began playing with fellow musicians Miles Davis and Thelonious Monk. They were also very much involved in creating different forms of jazz, Davis on the trumpet and Monk on the piano. Working with them, Coltrane learned to use tricks of phrasing and harmony to produce strange new sounds with his saxophone. His technique relied on rapid runs that made it almost impossible to tell one note from another. This revolutionary style became known as "sheets of sound." It was very controversial in the music world, and some people had a hard time accepting it as jazz. To many of them, the sounds Coltrane produced clashed instead of harmonized.

In 1960, with McCoy Tyner on piano, Elvin Jones on drums, and Jimmy Garrison on bass, Coltrane formed his own quartet. He released his most famous piece, "My Favorite Things," during this period. He also continued to experiment and improvise with both meter and the musical scale. By the mid-1960s, Coltrane was one of the most famous living jazz legends, with fans in Europe and Japan as well as at home.

September 21. President Lyndon Johnson named Walter Washington, an African American, the first mayor of Washington, D.C. At the time of his nomination to head the nation's largest predominately black city, Washington was chairman of the New York City Housing Authority.

1968

January 16. Lucius D. Amerson began serving as sheriff of Macon County, Alabama, making him the first black sheriff in the South since Reconstruction. Three new deputies, one white and two blacks, were sworn in with Amerson.

February 8. South Carolina law enforcement officers killed three black students and wounded several others during a disturbance on the campus of South Carolina State College at Orangeburg.

The trouble began as a protest against segregation at a local bowling alley. National Guard troops were eventually called out to restore order, and some students were jailed on charges of trespassing. In addition, school officials shut down the college for two weeks.

The February 8 incident occurred after someone knocked down and injured a state trooper with a piece of wood. The U.S. Justice Department looked into the matter and later filed a lawsuit against the owners of the segregated bowling alley, charging them with violation of the Civil Rights Act of 1964. Similar suits were also filed against Orangeburg hospitals for segregation and discrimination. The courts upheld the antisegregation complaints in both cases. However, authorities were unsuccessful in their attempts to bring the law enforcement officers involved in the shooting to trial.

The funeral procession of Martin Luther King, Jr.

March 2. The Kerner Commission passed along to President Lyndon Johnson the results of its investigation into the causes of the many civil disturbances that rocked the country during 1967.

In their report, members of the commission declared that "white racism" was the major cause of the 1967 riots. They also pointed out that the United States was well on its way to splitting into two communities, "one white, one black, separate and unequal." (Also see entry dated May 1-October 1, 1967.)

April 4. Martin Luther King, Jr., was assassinated in Memphis, Tennessee, by a white escaped convict named James Earl Ray. (See entries dated March 10, 1969; January 8, 1970; June 21, 1974; June 29, 1974; October 29, 1974; and February 28, 1975.) King had been in Memphis to support striking garbage workers. He had spoken to them at a rally just the day before he was shot.

In the days after King's death, racial rioting broke out in at least 125 towns and cities across the country. Hundreds of thousands of people attended his funeral services in Atlanta on April 9, and President Lyndon Johnson declared a day of national mourning. It was the most stately farewell ever given to an American civilian.

April 6. A gun battle between members of the Black Panthers and police in Oakland, California, resulted in the death of Panther Party member Bobby Hutton and the wounding of two policemen. Among the Panthers charged in connection with the shooting was Panther Minister of Information Eldridge Cleaver.

A native of Arkansas, Cleaver was born in 1935. During the late 1950s and early 1960s, he spent much of his time in various California prisons, where he earned his high school diploma and converted to the Black Muslim faith. He also began writing, and in 1968, he published a collection of essays entitled *Soul on Ice* that examined black attitudes toward American society. It became a bestseller and a minor classic in revolutionary literature.

Eldridge Cleaver

After Cleaver left prison, he went to work as a staff writer for *Ramparts* magazine and lectured on the black power movement at colleges and universities. Soon he became the chief spokesman for the Black Panther Party.

In 1969, facing yet another prison sentence for the Oakland shootout, Cleaver secretly left the United States. He headed first for Cuba and, after a few other stops, eventually ended up in Algeria, where the government had given the Panthers the status of a "liberation movement." (Also see entry dated November 19, 1975.)

April 11. President Lyndon Johnson signed the Fair Housing Act, also known as the Civil Rights Act of 1968. It banned racial discrimination in the sale and rental of most housing units in the country.

Resurrection City

May 11. Ralph Abernathy, who had replaced Martin Luther King, Jr., as head of the Southern Christian Leadership Conference (SCLC), led a group of blacks, poor whites, Native Americans, and Mexican Americans to Washington, D.C., for the so-called "Poor People's Campaign."

The marchers built dozens of plywood shacks on a campsite not far from the White House that they named Resurrection City. Meanwhile, their leaders tried to pressure Congress and the president to take action to eliminate poverty in the United States. But the government was more concerned with the war in Vietnam at the time, so the demonstrators' demands were mostly ignored. Bad weather and a lack of cooking, bathing, and sanitation facilities forced most people out of Resurrection City before the end of June.

July 23-24. A serious racial disturbance in Cleveland, Ohio, left three white police officers and eight black people dead.

It began when a small band of armed "Black Nationalists" started fighting Cleveland police in the Glenville ghetto. Widespread burning and looting followed, resulting in an estimated $1.5 million in property damage.

September 8. After a controversial trial, Black Panther leader Huey Newton was convicted of manslaughter for killing a policeman in Oakland, California, in 1967. He had also been connected with the wounding of another policeman and the kidnapping of a black motorist.

In his defense, Newton had claimed that he was unconscious from a gunshot wound at the time the policeman was shot. His trial attracted more than 2,500 demonstrators,

Shirley Chisholm

many of whom shouted their support for both the Panthers and Newton. (Also see entries dated May 29, 1970; August, 1970; August 8, 1971; December 15, 1971; November 2, 1974; and August 22, 1989.)

November 5. New York's Shirley Chisholm defeated former CORE chairman James Farmer for a seat in the U.S. House of Representatives, becoming the first black woman ever to serve in Congress.

Born in Brooklyn, New York, in 1924, Chisholm grew up on the Caribbean island of Barbados in the home of her maternal grandmother. She received her early education in the British-style schools on the island, then returned to New York in 1934 and completed her studies there.

After graduating from Brooklyn College, Chisholm taught school for several years and worked on her master's degree at Columbia University. She also became interested in politics around this same time and worked behind the scenes in local Democratic activities. Her own career as a public servant began in 1964 when she was elected to the New York State Assembly.

Four years later, Chisholm took on a new challenge—serving in the U.S. House of Representatives. There she established a reputation as a feisty and independent legislator who devoted her efforts to working for the poor and on issues involving women and children. (Also see entries dated January 25, 1972; July 12, 1972; and February 10, 1982.)

December 31. Lyndon Johnson ended his last full year in office having named more blacks to high-level federal positions than any previous president. Just before leaving the White House, he appointed five black ambassadors, promoted Wade McCree from the U.S. District Court to a Court of Appeals judgeship, named Hobart Taylor to the Board of the Export-Import Bank, and made Andrew Brimmer a governor of the Federal Reserve Board.

1969   **January 8.** At predominately white Brandeis University in Waltham, Massachusetts, sixty-five black students invaded Ford Hall, the campus communications center, and barricaded themselves in the building. They then presented school officials with a "nonnegotiable" list of demands.

Among these demands were the creation of an African studies department, year-round recruitment of black students by blacks, the naming of black directors to head the Upward Bound and Transitional Year programs, the hiring of black professors, the establishment of an Afro-American student center, and the funding of ten full scholarships for blacks. Morris B. Abram, the university's new president, offered the demonstrators a temporary pardon and agreed to talk with them.

January 25. A mistrial was declared in the Mississippi murder trial of Ku Klux Klan leader Samuel H. Bowers, Jr.

Bowers was one of thirteen men charged with the 1966 firebomb slaying of black civil rights leader Vernon Dahmer. The thirteen were tried separately. Four were convicted of murder and sentenced to prison. Five cases—including Bowers's—ended in mistrials when juries were unable to reach verdicts. In May, 1968, an arson case against Bowers that was connected to the Dahmer murder also ended in a mistrial.

Many observers believed that these efforts to prosecute white men who had committed brutal acts against blacks were partly responsible for discouraging additional racial violence in Mississippi and the rest of the South.

January-March. Richard M. Nixon, elected president without much black support, named only three blacks to top-level jobs in his administration. He made James Farmer the assistant secretary of health, education and welfare, Arthur A. Fletcher the assistant secretary of labor, and William H. Brown III the chairman of the Equal Employment Opportunity Commission (EEOC).

March 10. Escaped convict James Earl Ray pleaded guilty to assassinating civil rights leader Martin Luther King, Jr., in Memphis, Tennessee, in 1968. He was sentenced to ninety-nine years in prison. (Also see entries dated April 4, 1968; January 8, 1970; June 21, 1974; June 29, 1974; October 29, 1974; and February 28, 1975.)

August 19. The FBI arrested Black Panther leader Bobby Seale in California for the torture-murder of fellow Panther Alex Rackley.

Rackley was burned to death on May 19, 1969, in New Haven, Connecticut, supposedly because he had been working as a police informant. Seale's attorney charged that the arrest was part of an organized campaign by the U.S. Justice

Department to harass the Black Panther Party. Seven other party members were also charged in Rackley's death, including Lonnie McLucas, the first to stand trial for the murder. (Also see entries dated August 31, 1970, and May 25, 1971.)

October 29. In the case of *Alexander v. Holmes,* the U.S. Supreme Court rejected the Nixon administration's appeal for a delay in desegregating thirty Mississippi school districts. The Court also ruled unanimously that school districts must immediately end racial segregation.

This decision indicated that the Court had finally given up on the idea of allowing desegregation to proceed "with all deliberate speed" as ordered in the famous *Brown v. Board of Education of Topeka, Kansas* case. (See entry dated May 31, 1955.) Courts across the country immediately began taking steps to force reluctant school systems to come up with desegregation plans and put them into effect.

December 4-5. Illinois Black Panther Party leaders Mark Clark and Fred Hampton were killed on December 4 when police raided an apartment near party headquarters in Chicago. Four other people, including two women, were wounded, and a total of seven Panthers were arrested.

Police had scheduled the pre-dawn raid after they heard that Hampton's apartment was being used to stockpile weapons. They claimed that their knock on the door was answered by shotgun fire from a woman, touching off a ten-minute fight during which about 200 shots were fired. On December 5, spokesmen for the Black Panthers rejected the police accounts of the raid and insisted that police had done all of the shooting and had "murdered" Clark and Hampton in bed.

Despite state, federal, and congressional investigations into the controversial encounter, no Panther members or police officers were ever brought to trial. However, the incident increased tensions between the Panthers and law enforcement organizations and helped the Panthers gain sympathy from many Americans.

1970   **January 5-7.** Black children enrolled in formerly all-white public schools in three districts in Mississippi as federal marshals watched.

The marshals had been sent to the state to prevent violence and to look for signs that officials were not obeying court orders to desegregate. There was no violence on the first day of classes, but many white parents picketed or boycotted the newly desegregated schools. In some districts, they objected to plans that involved busing children to schools that were far from their homes.

January 8. The Tennessee Supreme Court refused to consider granting a new trial to James Earl Ray, convicted assassin of civil rights leader Martin Luther King, Jr. The court declared there was no reason to order a new trial for a man who had pleaded guilty to the crime and who understood what he was doing when he entered his plea. (Also see entries dated April 4, 1968; March 10, 1969; June 21, 1974; June 29, 1974; October 29, 1974; and February 28, 1975.)

January 15. Blacks and whites across the nation celebrated the forty-first anniversary of the birth of Martin Luther King, Jr., as the movement to make the day a national holiday gained support in several states and major cities.

Following a memorial service in Atlanta, Georgia, King's widow, Coretta Scott King, dedicated the new Martin Luther King, Jr., Memorial Center. It included the slain civil rights leader's birthplace, church, and tomb.

February 1. School officials in twenty districts in Alabama, Georgia, and Mississippi defied federal court orders and refused to desegregate their schools. Some administrators closed their schools temporarily while others supported boycotts by white parents and students.

February 28. A confidential memo from President Richard Nixon's domestic advisor, Daniel P. Moynihan, was made public and immediately created a controversy.

In his memo, Moynihan, known as a liberal Democrat, proposed that "the time may have come when the issue of race could benefit from a period of 'benign neglect.'" He later explained that all he meant was that conditions would improve for blacks if extremists on both sides of the political spectrum would lower their voices. He insisted that he had two reasons for writing the memo: to bring the president up to date on the "quite extraordinary" progress of blacks in the last decade, and to suggest ways in which these gains could be "consolidated" in the future.

On March 5, twenty black civil rights leaders, authors, legislators, and educators issued a statement describing Moynihan's memo as "symptomatic of a calculated, aggressive and systematic" effort by the Nixon administration to "wipe out" nearly two decades of civil rights progress.

April 8. In a major defeat for the Nixon administration, the U.S. Senate voted to reject the president's nomination of G. Harrold Carswell to the U.S. Supreme Court. The NAACP had spoken out against Carswell because of his pro-segregation record.

March 3. A mob of angry whites carrying ax handles and baseball bats stormed buses transporting black school children to a formerly all-white school in Lamar, South Carolina.

About 100 South Carolina state troopers broke up the crowd with riot clubs and tear gas after about 200 white men and women rushed the buses and smashed the windows at Lamar High School. Several children received minor injuries from flying glass and the effects of tear gas.

Although no one was arrested at the scene, the mob's leaders were later picked up by state and federal officials. In February, 1971, a county grand jury charged twenty-two of the whites with rioting in connection with the incident. The grand jury dropped charges against twenty-one other whites, including a state legislator.

March 13. The U.S. Senate voted to extend the Voting Rights Act of 1965 until 1975. It established that a person did not have to pass a reading and writing test in order to vote. It also gave a person permission to vote in presidential elections if he could prove that he had lived in a district at least a month before election day.

May 12. Six black men died as a result of racial rioting in Augusta, Georgia. All were killed by local police.

May 14. Mississippi law enforcement officers killed two black youths during a racial disturbance at Jackson State College. The officers were not charged with any crime.

May 29. The California Court of Appeals overturned Black Panther leader Huey

Newton's 1968 manslaughter conviction for killing a policeman in Oakland, California, in 1967. The Appeals Court ruled that the jury in Newton's trial had not received proper instructions from the judge. (Also see entries dated September 8, 1968; August, 1970; August 8, 1971; December 15, 1971; November 2, 1974; and August 22, 1989.)

July 7-31. Racial rioting occurred in several northern cities.

The resort town of Asbury Park, New Jersey, experienced four days of violence during which forty-three people were shot. Calm returned after the town's mayor agreed to consider a list of twenty-two demands that a group of black organizations presented to him. These demands included requests for better housing, more jobs, and increased efforts to stop drug traffic.

A few days later, New Bedford, Massachusetts, was the scene of four nights of racial disturbances. And at the end of the month, African Americans and Puerto Ricans rioted in Hartford, Connecticut, for three days.

August 7. Four people died during a shootout at the Marin County (California) Courthouse when three black convicts (including the so-called "Soledad Brothers") tried to escape. A judge, two of the convicts, and another black youth who was helping the convicts were killed.

The Soledad Brothers—Fleeta Drumgo and John Cluchette—were black inmates at California's Soledad Prison who had been accused of killing a guard along with another man named George Jackson. Their case became a cause for many

Angela Davis

black and white radicals who insisted that the blacks had been set up.

One of their most outspoken defenders was a young black woman named Angela Davis. She was a scholar and political activist who had been fired from her teaching job at the University of California in Los Angeles because she was a member of the Communist party. Davis owned the guns used in the courtroom shootout, which was enough to land her on the FBI's "Ten Most Wanted" list for helping to plot the attempted escape. To avoid being captured, she left California and secretly made her way across the country. (Also see entries dated October 13, 1970; January 5, 1971; and June 4, 1972.)

August 17. James A. Alfonso, a member of the city of Chicago's police gang intelligence unit, died from wounds he received on August 13 when someone fired a shot into his unmarked police car. He was the fourth police officer killed in the city's black neighborhoods since mid-June. The next day, Chicago police said that they had arrested several members of the "Main 21," the ruling body of the Black P. Stone Nation, a confederation of sixty black street gangs.

The alleged involvement of black gangs in the murder increased tensions between the black community and Chicago police. Some blacks charged that the violence resulted from a widespread pattern of police brutality and a series of incidents in which the police had killed blacks, including members of the Black Panther Party. (Also see entry dated January 17, 1971.)

August 27. David L. Rice, minister of information for a branch of the Black Panther Party called the National Committee to Combat Fascism (NCCF), surrendered to police in Omaha, Nebraska, in connection with the August 17 death of a local policeman.

Officer Larry D. Minard was killed when he touched a suitcase that was filled with an explosive and rigged as a booby trap. Seven other Omaha police officers were also injured. The eight officers had responded to a call in a predominately black neighborhood to investigate a report of a woman in distress.

At first, Rice was just charged with illegal possession of explosives. But on October 28, he and another NCCF leader, Edward A. Poindexter, were ordered to stand trial on murder charges.

August 29-31. In Philadelphia, Pennsylvania, one police officer was killed and six others were wounded in a series of gun battles between police and members of several black militant organizations, including the Black Panthers.

The clashes began after police raided the Panther Information Center in search of a suspect they believed was connected to an earlier shooting. Police Commissioner Frank Rizzo blamed the incidents on a group called "The Revolutionaries," which he said had plotted to murder police officers, and the local Black Panther Party.

August 31. More than 200 school districts across the South that had resisted desegregation since the U.S. Supreme Court Order in 1954 reopened peacefully with newly desegregated classrooms. However, 175 other districts continued to hold out for segregation. Most of these were involved in court cases on the controversial issue of student busing.

August 31. Black Panther Lonnie McLucas was convicted of conspiracy to murder in the 1969 torture-murder of a fellow Panther, Alex Rackley. McLucas was later sentenced to serve twelve to fifteen years in prison. His attorney argued that another Panther, George Sams, Jr., had actually given the order to torture and kill Rackley. (Also see entries dated August 19, 1969, and May 25, 1971.)

August. Black Panther leader Huey Newton was released on bond to wait for a new trial on the charge of killing an Oakland, California, policeman in 1967. He had already been convicted of manslaughter in the case in September, 1968, but the California Appeals Court overturned the conviction in May, 1970. At the time of his release, Newton had already served more than two years in jail during his first trial and the appeals process. (Also see entries dated September 8, 1968; May 29, 1970; August 8, 1971; December 15, 1971; November 2, 1974; and August 22, 1989.)

September 1. A federal grand jury in Augusta, Georgia, charged two white police officers with violating the civil rights of two black men who were shot May 12 during a night of rioting that left six blacks dead and sixty others injured. Georgia governor Lester Maddox condemned the decision to try the police officers, declaring that the "national government, from the President on down, is only worrying about agitators."

September 5-7. The Black Panther Party and members of the Women's Liberation Movement and the Gay Liberation Movement opened their "Revolutionary People's Constitutional Convention" in Philadelphia, Pennsylvania. About 6,000 people attended. Members of the Panther Party had organized the convention in order to rewrite the U.S. Constitution because they felt it did not fully protect the rights of oppressed people.

September 9. Another round of school desegregation in the South began. Unlike the peaceful opening of schools on August 31, this opening was marked by stiffening white resistance to federal orders and confusion over which schools students had been assigned to and how busing was being handled.

September 14-15. One black youth was killed and twenty-one others were injured during a day-long gun battle between police and blacks in a New Orleans housing project.

The incident began on September 14 when members of the National Committee to Combat Fascism (NCCF) found out that two black undercover police officers were working within the organization. They beat the policemen and then turned them over to a crowd of about 100 blacks for a "people's trial," but the officers managed to escape.

Later, police and fire fighters returned to the housing project to investigate reports of a burning car. Shots were fired at them, and the riot broke out in full force. Fourteen blacks, most of them from the NCCF, were arrested and charged with attempted murder. (Also see entry dated August 6, 1971.)

October 5-November 8. Violent racial clashes connected with school desegregation occurred in three cities in both the North and South.

Four white boys and one black youth were shot and wounded in two apparently related incidents on October 5 and 7 outside a desegregated high school in Pontiac, Michigan. Also on October 7, a second black student was struck down by a car near Pontiac Central High School as white and black students threw rocks and bottles at each other. Tensions had run high in Pontiac ever since a court ordered the city's public schools to desegregate.

Public schools in Trenton, New Jersey, were closed on October 29 and 30 after the school board's decision to begin busing students to achieve racial balance led to violence. The trouble started when scuffles broke out between 100 black and white students in a predominantly Italian section of the city. The fighting then spread into the downtown area when bands of black youths flooded the streets and threw bottles at police officers and broke windows. More than 200 people were arrested during the three days of disorder.

On November 5 through 8 in Henderson, North Carolina, a clash between blacks and the county school board over school desegregation policies touched off four days of occasional sniper fire and burnings. Police jailed 101 people during the disturbance. Blacks in Henderson had been protesting for a long time against the school board's decision to reopen an all-black school in the community. They felt that school officials were just looking for a way to avoid desegregation. The protest ended in violence, and the National Guard was called to help restore order. By November 9, the school board had agreed to close the all-black school and bus its students to desegregated schools.

October 12-14. The U.S. Supreme Court heard arguments on student busing and racial balance in southern schools, specifically in the districts of Charlotte, North Carolina, and Mobile, Alabama.

Attorneys for the NAACP Legal Defense and Educational Fund represented black children in the hearings. They argued that each black child had a constitutional right to be enrolled in a school that was not recognizably black. They also insisted that any desegregation plan that did not eliminate every all-black school should be considered inadequate. The NAACP lawyers told the court that allowing some southern districts to have recognizably black school undermined the *Brown v. Board of Education of Topeka, Kansas* decision of 1954. (See entry dated May 17, 1954.)

Solicitor General Ervin N. Griswold, representing the U.S. Justice Department, argued that the NAACP's request amounted to a demand for racial balance in the schools, something the Constitution did not require. Lawyers for the school districts maintained that court-ordered desegregation plans assigning children to schools by race also violated the *Brown* decision. Furthermore, they said, the busing of schoolchildren to increase desegregation was unconstitutional.

After hearing all of these arguments, the Supreme Court promised to issue its ruling soon.

October 13. FBI agents arrested black revolutionary Angela Davis after tracing her to a New York City motel.

Davis had been on the FBI's "Ten Most Wanted" list ever since August, when she was allegedly involved in a courtroom shootout and the attempted escape of three black convicts in California. The shootout resulted in the death of a judge and three other men. (Also see entries dated August 7, 1970; January 5, 1971; and June 4, 1972.)

October 19. At the request of the U.S. Attorney in Chicago, Illinois, U.S. District Court Judge Julius J. Hoffman dismissed conspiracy charges against Bobby Seale, chairman of the Black Panther Party.

Seale was one of eight men charged with conspiracy to riot at the 1968 Democratic National Convention in Chicago. Judge Hoffman had separated Seale's case from that of the other seven (all of whom were white) after the Black Panther leader had bitterly criticized the way the judge was handling the trial. (In fact, all eight defendants and their lawyers made fun of Judge Hoffman throughout the trial to show how ridiculous they thought it was.)

The seven whites (popularly known as the "Chicago Seven") were eventually found not guilty of the conspiracy to riot charges. The U.S. Attorney then asked Judge Hoffman to drop similar charges against Seale, too, saying that "it would be inappropriate to try [him] alone." Like the other seven, Seale had also faced contempt charges for his actions in the courtroom, but those were eventually dropped, too.

October 24-25. Violent clashes between blacks and police officers continued in northern ghettoes.

In Cairo, Illinois, on the night of October 24, a white-owned grocery store across from an all-black housing project was set on fire. Later that evening and into the early hours of October 25, several carloads of armed blacks riddled the local police station with hundreds of rounds of gunfire three times in six hours. No police officers were wounded, and they managed to drive away the attackers after each assault.

On October 24 in Detroit, one black police officer was killed and another wounded in a shooting at the headquarters of the National Committee to Combat Fascism. After a day-long confrontation around the NCCF offices, fifteen blacks—seven men and eight women—were arrested and charged with murder and conspiracy. The NCCF claimed that the disturbance began after two policemen beat two youths who were selling Black Panther Party literature on a Detroit street corner. The NCCF also insisted that police fired the first shots. (Also see entry dated June 30, 1971.)

November 20-22. More than 500 inmates reportedly took part in a racial disturbance at the huge Cumming prison farm about 90 miles southeast of Little Rock, Arkansas.

Inmates had demanded separate living quarters for black and white prisoners, which touched off a fight. When the violence turned into a near-riot, state troopers were called in to help restore order. Prison guards eventually broke up the fighting with tear gas.

1971   **January 4.** Leon Howard Sullivan, pastor of Philadelphia's Zion Baptist Church and founder of Opportunities Industrialization Centers of America (OIC), a job-training program for blacks and other minorities, was elected to the board of directors of the General Motors Corporation (GM).

Sullivan had first received national attention in 1963. As a young minister, he had increased his church's membership from 600 to 5,000. He also established a day care center, a federal credit union, a community center, an employment agency, adult education reading classes, several athletic teams, choral groups, and a family counseling service. For these and other accomplishments, *Life* magazine named Sullivan one of 100 outstanding young adults in the United States in 1963.

A year later, Sullivan established the first Opportunities Industrialization Center in an abandoned jailhouse in Philadelphia, Pennsylvania. Starting with almost nothing, he built OIC into a multi-million-dollar enterprise that has trained and found jobs for more than 200,000 people. Studies have shown that the OIC programs are cheaper than many other similar programs and that they are more effective than vocational education programs in the nation's high schools.

Many people interpreted Sullivan's election to the GM board as a way for the company to satisfy increasing demands to give the public and minority groups a voice in corporate decision-making. At GM's annual stockholders' meeting in May, 1970, a reform group called the Project on Corporate Responsibility had criticized the company for not having a black director on its board.

January 5. In California, Angela Davis was brought before a judge and officially charged with murder, kidnapping, and conspiracy for her part in a 1970 courtroom shootout that left four men dead. Denied bail because of the seriousness of the charges against her, Davis remained in jail for sixteen months until her case finally came to trial in the spring of 1972. (Also see entries dated August 7, 1970; October 13, 1970; and June 4, 1972.)

January 11. The U.S. Supreme Court agreed to review the 1967 draft evasion conviction of former heavyweight boxing champion Muhammad Ali.

Ali had been convicted when the courts rejected his argument that he should be excused from the draft because he was a Black Muslim minister. Because of his opposition to the Vietnam War, he was also stripped of his boxing titles and banned from the sport for awhile. In 1969, however, the Supreme Court ruled that conscientious objectors could base their claims on philosophical or moral objections as well as strictly religious grounds. So Ali decided to appeal.

By agreeing to review his case, the Supreme Court guaranteed that Ali would be free to fight the recognized title holder, Joe Frazier, in March. (Also see entries dated March 8, 1971, and June 28, 1971.)

January 14. The U.S. Supreme Court ruled that southern states must obtain federal approval before making any changes in their election laws that might affect the rights of black voters as outlined in the 1965 Voting Rights Act.

January 17. In Chicago, Illinois, a jury made up of blacks and whites acquitted seven members of the Black P. Stone Nation on charges that they had murdered a Chicago policeman in 1970. Their alleged involvement in the shooting had greatly increased tensions between police and the black community in Chicago. (Also see entry dated August 17, 1970.)

February 6-9. National Guard troops patrolled the streets of Wilmington, North Carolina, after four days of racial violence that left two people dead.

The unrest was linked to the city's school desegregation plans and black students' boycott of the local high school. Local officers, helped by the National Guard troops, restored order on February 8 but remained on alert.

March 8. Files stolen from an FBI office in Media, Pennsylvania, that were released to the public revealed that the U.S. government was actively investigating black activist groups, especially the Black Student Union movement.

The Black Student Unions and other similar organizations had begun springing up on predominantly white college campuses during the late 1960s as black enrollments increased. Some of these black students encountered what they felt was bias against them, and they held protests that sometimes bordered on violence. The FBI feared that such students might fall under the influence and control of "extremists" like the Black Panthers.

March 8. In New York City, Joe Frazier defeated challenger Muhammad Ali to retain the world heavyweight boxing championship. (Also see entries dated January 11, 1971, and June 28, 1971.)

March 11. Whitney M. Young, Jr., executive director of the National Urban League, drowned while swimming in Nigeria. Young and a group of other Americans, white and black, had been in the city of Lagos attending a conference. The goal of the conference was to bridge the gap between Africans and Americans, particularly black Americans.

Born in Kentucky in 1922, Young was educated at Kentucky State College, the Massachusetts Institute of Technology, and the University of Minnesota, from which he received a master's degree in social work in 1947. From 1954 until 1961, he was head of the School of Social Work at Atlanta University.

Young left Atlanta University to become executive director of the National Urban League, the country's leading black economic and social reform agency. There he worked hard to establish connections with white business and political leaders that he thought would lead to more jobs for blacks.

Some members of the black community condemned him for this and called him an "Uncle Tom," a put-down term used to describe a black person who is eager to win the approval of whites. ("Uncle Tom" was a character in Harriet Beecher Stowe's antislavery novel *Uncle Tom's Cabin*.) But Young was an outspoken critic of businesses and government agencies that he thought were moving too slowly to improve life for black people. He made the Urban League more effective and increased its influence. During the height of the civil rights era, Young was one of the movement's "Big Four" leaders. The others were Martin Luther King, Jr., Roy

Wilkins, and James Farmer.

March 23. Walter E. Fauntroy, a Baptist clergyman and a Democrat, was elected the District of Columbia's first congressional delegate in the twentieth century. Because of Washington's special status as a federal district rather than a full-fledged city or state, Fauntroy could vote in certain committees but was not allowed to vote on the House floor.

March 25. President Richard Nixon met with the Congressional Black Caucus (a group of black members of the U.S. House of Representatives) to receive a list of sixty complaints presented on behalf of black Americans.

The meeting had first been suggested back in 1969. It was finally set up not long after Caucus members boycotted President Nixon's State of the Union Address in January, 1971. The group charged that the president's failure to meet with them up until that time showed how little he cared about the opinions of black Americans.

At the meeting, the black representatives asked for reforms in areas such as welfare, job discrimination and job placement, social justice, and school desegregation. The president responded by naming five White House staff members to work on a list of recommendations.

On May 18, President Nixon presented a report outlining the steps his administration would be willing to take to help black Americans. In almost every instance, he disagreed with the Caucus about the amount of money the government should spend on reform programs and how comprehensive those programs should be. After studying the list, the Black Caucus expressed "deep disappointment" over the president's "lack of understanding, urgency and commitment in dealing with the critical problems facing black Americans."

April 20. The U.S. Supreme Court ruled in four separate cases that busing children to achieve school desegregation was constitutional. The Court made it clear, however, that the rulings did not apply to segregation caused by neighborhood housing patterns, as is found most often in the North.

The landmark decision has become known to history as *Swann v. Charlotte-Mecklenburg*. It ended the efforts of southern school boards to prevent forced busing through legal means.

May 5. A riot involving mostly black youths occurred in the Brownsville (Brooklyn) section of New York City.

The disturbance began after thousands of angry Brownsville residents closed off streets in their neighborhood with abandoned cars and trash piles to protest state budget cuts affecting welfare and food stamp assistance, anti-drug programs, Medicaid, and educational facilities. What was intended as a peaceful protest turned violent after groups of young people set fires, looted stores, and battled police with rocks, bricks, and bottles. One officer was shot and fourteen others were injured during the disturbance, and twenty-five people were arrested. Organizers of the protest condemned the actions of the rioting youths, and police were able to bring things under control by late evening.

May 21-26. Racial violence erupted in Chattanooga, Tennessee, after a black musician failed to perform at a rock concert in the city auditorium. When some of the black youths did not get the ticket refunds they felt they deserved, they began vandalizing the building. The disorder later spread into the streets.

On May 24, the governor sent 2,000 National Guard troops to the city after local police were unable to stop the arson and sniper fire in the black neighborhoods near the downtown area. The next day, police shot and killed a young black man they said had been throwing bricks at them. Black witnesses said the man was apparently drunk and that he had not given the police any reason to shoot him. The incident increased tensions, but it did not lead to more violence.

On May 26, authorities lifted a rigid dusk-to-dawn curfew, and the governor announced that he would gradually withdraw the National Guard troops.

May 25. Racial tension was sparked again in the South after Jo Etha Collier, an eighteen-year-old black girl, was shot dead in her hometown of Drew, Mississippi.

Less than an hour after she had graduated from desegregated Drew High School, Collier was struck by a bullet from a passing car as she stood with other young blacks on a street corner. On May 26, police arrested three white men and charged them with the killing. They were brought up before a judge on June 14, at which time they pleaded innocent. But the swift arrests as well as the sympathetic attitude of local white officials helped calm tensions in the community.

May 25. A judge in Connecticut dismissed all charges against Black Panthers Bobby Seale and Ericka Huggins in connection with the 1969 torture-murder of another Panther, Alex Rackley.

Eight Panthers had originally been charged for taking part in Rackley's murder. At Seale's trial in early 1971, one of the others who had been accused, George Sams, Jr., insisted that Seale had actually given the order to torture and kill Rackley. (Sams had already pleaded guilty to second-degree murder at his own trial and had agreed to testify against Seale.) But after the jury was unable to reach a verdict in Seale's case, the judge declared a mistrial and announced that "massive publicity" had made it too difficult to find an unbiased jury to try Seale and Huggins a second time. (Also see entries dated August 19, 1969, and August 31, 1970.)

May 30. Three police officers were injured in a gun battle in Cairo, Illinois, one of the most racially tense cities in America. The mayor blamed the shootings on the United Front, a predominantly black organization that had led a boycott of the town's white merchants. The United Front refused to comment on the shooting.

June 2. Samuel L. Gravely, Jr., was named the first black admiral in the U.S. Navy. He served as director of naval communications in Washington, D.C.

June 4-22. Racial tensions in Columbus, Georgia, the state's second largest city, erupted into violence.

The trouble began on May 31, 1971, when seven policemen who were members of the African-American Police League were fired for picketing police headquarters and allegedly "ripping" the American flag patches from their uniforms. They had been protesting alleged racial discrimination in the police department.

On June 3, a county grand jury announced that complaints of discrimination against black officers were untrue. The jury had also looked into charges of police brutality in the arrests of black people but found no evidence to support such claims.

On June 19, Hosea Williams, national program director for the Southern Christian Leadership Conference (SCLC) and chairman of a statewide group called the Black Leadership Coalition, led more than 500 blacks on a fifteen-block march in Columbus. He then presented a list of five demands to city and county officials. The

Coalition insisted that thirteen black policemen who had been removed from their jobs be returned to the force. The group also demanded that thirty-eight blacks still on the force be promoted and that more black police officers be hired. Finally, they called for the desegregation of jail facilities and the creation of a biracial "citizens police review board."

On June 21, the mayor of Columbus declared a state of emergency following a weekend of racial conflict, including twenty-six arson fires and the fatal shooting of a black man by police. The city council gave the mayor broad powers to order a curfew, shut down stores selling alcoholic beverages, stop the sale of firearms, and cut back on gasoline sales.

Meanwhile, the African-American Police League called for a city-wide boycott of white businesses. Later in the month, white police officers presented a petition to the mayor urging him not to give in to black demands.

June 13. The latest in a series of race riots on military bases occurred in Texas at Sheppard Air Force Base. A nighttime battle between white and black airmen left twenty injured.

According to a military spokesman, the trouble started when one black airman and one white airman clashed in the base's club. Then young trainees became involved. It took base police more than two hours to bring things under control.

June 15. Vernon E. Jordan, Jr., a former attorney in Atlanta, Georgia, and executive director of the United Negro College Fund (UNCF), was named executive director of the National Urban League (NUL). Jordan replaced Whitney Young, Jr., who had died three months before in Lagos, Nigeria. (See entry dated March 11, 1971.)

Vernon Jordan

Born in Atlanta in 1935, Jordan received his education at De Pauw University and Howard University Law School. He then returned to Georgia to work as a civil rights lawyer and as an official of the state branch of the NAACP. From 1964 until 1969, Jordan was director of the Voter Education Project (VEP) of the Southern Regional Council. As head of the VEP, he helped organize massive voter registration campaigns across the South to help blacks win political power.

In January, 1970, Jordan became head of the UNCF, which raises funds for more than thirty black colleges across the country. He left there to head the National Urban League, where he earned a reputation as an energetic and innovative leader with his programs to increase voter registration in the North and the West. He also spoke out forcefully on a number of employment issues that were of vital importance to the black community. (Also see entries dated May 29, 1980, and November 3, 1992.)

June 17. Police officers armed with riot equipment broke up a crowd of 400 black youths in a second night of racial violence in Jacksonville, Florida.

The rioters were angry about an earlier incident in which police killed a young black man. After the youths began throwing rocks and bottles and set two supermarkets on fire in a black neighborhood, police moved in to protect the many elderly people who lived there. The disturbance left several police officers with slight injuries, and three young people were arrested for looting.

June 25. Agents from the Bureau of Alcohol, Tobacco, and Firearms (ATF) arrested three black men in Columbus, Georgia, and charged them with possessing firebombs in the racially tense city.

The ATF agents said that the three men had stockpiled enough material at the People's Panther Party headquarters to make more than fifty firebombs. (The People's Panther Party was reportedly a training group for the Black Panther Party.) Two of the three men were soldiers stationed at nearby Fort Benning, and the third was a former Army private.

Their arrests came less than a week after the outbreak of new racial disorders, which included firebombings.

June 28. The U.S. Supreme Court overturned boxer Muhammad Ali's 1967 conviction for draft evasion. The justices based their ruling on the grounds that Ali's Black Muslim beliefs were sincere and that he should have been excused from military service because of those beliefs. (Also see entry dated January 11, 1971.)

June 30. In Detroit, Michigan, a jury made up of blacks and whites found twelve members of the National Committee to Combat Fascism (NCCF) not guilty of killing a police officer and wounding another during a 1970 shootout at NCCF headquarters. Three other members, however, were convicted of assault for the shootings. (Also see entry dated October 24-25, 1970.)

July 6. Black jazz trumpeter Louis Armstrong died in New York. During his long and hugely successful career, he reshaped the development of American music by introducing the sounds of black folk music from New Orleans into the mainstream culture.

Born around 1900, "Satchmo" Armstrong grew up in the slums of his native New Orleans, Louisiana. A run-in with the law when he was thirteen landed him in a juvenile home, where he learned to play the cornet (a type of trumpet) and discovered his talent for imitating the popular songs of the day just by listening to them. (He never did learn to read music.) He was also a very inventive musician who could add surprising twists and turns to a melody as he played it.

Louis Armstrong

When he was still just a teenager, Armstrong played with various bands in New Orleans nightclubs and on board Mississippi riverboat cruises. During the 1920s, he headed north, developing his skills as a jazz trumpeter first in Chicago, Illinois then in New York City. Returning to Chicago in late 1925, he formed his own band.

Up to that time, jazz was usually performed by a group of musicians, and no one took center stage. But Armstrong changed all that. Not only did he play his instrument like no one else, he also sang, danced, and did comedy routines. Audiences loved his spectacular trumpet solos and coarse, raspy voice, especially when he sang "scat." (Scat is a type of jazz singing in which a person makes up nonsense syllables and sounds to go along with the music. Armstrong is credited with inventing it.) Some recordings he made during this same period helped him become nationally famous, and by the end of the 1920s, he was the country's leading jazz musician.

Personal problems and money troubles led to a decline in Armstrong's popularity during the late 1930s and 1940s. But he slowly made his way to the top again during the late 1940s and 1950s with new recordings, tours, and appearances in movies and on television. Throughout the 1960s, he was one of the most famous and best-loved entertainers in the entire world. Poor health finally forced Armstrong to slow down as the 1970s began.

July 7. Professional baseball commissioner Bowie Kuhn announced that veteran black player Satchel Paige, who pitched for twenty-five years in the Negro Leagues and the Major Leagues, would be given full membership in the Baseball Hall of Fame at Cooperstown, New York.

Officials had originally planned to honor Paige and other black players in a separate division of the Hall of Fame established especially for players in the old Negro Leagues. Baseball fans criticized the idea, however, so officials decided to give Paige full honors.

July 21. Blacks in Passaic, New Jersey, began a long boycott against downtown merchants to protest alleged police brutality.

The boycott grew out of a series of incidents of alleged police harassment and brutality, including a fight on the night of July 20 between police and eight blacks that involved gunfire and the beating of a black man. Black leaders charged that the town's all-white city council ignored black pleas for protection against police harassment. The FBI agreed to investigate their claims.

August 6. In New Orleans, Louisiana, a jury made up of whites and blacks found twelve black members of the National Committee to Combat Fascism (NCCF) not guilty of attempted murder. The charges stemmed from a 1970 riot at a New Orleans housing project that included a day-long gun battle between police and NCCF members. (Also see entry dated September 14-15, 1970.)

August 8. Black Panther leader Huey Newton's second trial for manslaughter in the 1967 killing of an Oakland, California, policeman ended in a mistrial after the jury could not reach a verdict. (Also see entries dated September 8, 1968; May 29, 1970; August, 1970; December 15, 1971; November 2, 1974; and August 22, 1989.)

August 18. A policeman in Jackson, Mississippi, was shot and killed when he and other local authorities raided the headquarters of the Republic of New Africa (RNA), a black separatist group. Another Jackson policeman and an FBI agent were wounded during the twenty-minute gun battle. They had gone to the RNA offices to serve three RNA members with fugitive warrants.

Five days after the raid, eleven RNA members, including the president of the organization, Imari A. Obadele, were accused of murder in the death of the policeman. They were also charged with treason for taking up arms against the state of Mississippi.

Obadele expressed regret over the policeman's death but criticized the Jackson Police Department and the FBI for raiding the office in the first place. He declared that his group would have accepted the fugitive warrants peacefully if one or two black lawyers had been there. In October, 1973, Obadele and six other RNA members were convicted of illegal possession of weapons and assault on a federal officer and sentenced to prison for terms ranging from three to twelve years.

August 18-September 13. As the fall school term approached, more legal fights over desegregation took place across the South in Alabama, Texas, Tennessee, and Virginia. But when schools began opening in late August and early September, the strongest opposition to court-ordered racial desegregation occurred in the North and West.

Alabama mothers opposed to busing meet with Governor George Wallace (left)

In Pontiac, Michigan, for example, eight white students and one black pupil were injured on September 8 as fights erupted during protests against a school busing plan. White parents—carrying American flags—marched in front of the school bus depot and dared bus drivers to run them down. About a week earlier, arsonists had used firebombs to destroy ten school buses that were going to be used to carry out desegregation plans. These protests in Pontiac were among the most violent in the country.

In San Francisco, California, Chinese Americans announced that they intended to resist a court-ordered busing plan that was supposed to go into effect on September 13. When that day arrived, nearly half the schoolchildren in the city stayed home in protest.

And in Boston, Massachusetts, parents of about 300 children who were assigned to a new racially desegregated school refused to enroll them there. Instead, the children returned to their old neighborhood schools. A similar protest occurred in Evansville, Indiana.

August 31. Warren E. Burger, Chief Justice of the U.S. Supreme Court, announced that he was afraid federal judges were misinterpreting the high Court's decision on busing that was delivered on April 20, 1971.

Burger said that judges were assuming the order *required* racial balance in every school. He explained that what he and his fellow justices really meant was that a judge could look at a school's racial balance—among other things—to help determine whether the law against segregated schools was being violated.

September 13. More than 1,000 state troopers, prison guards, and sheriff's deputies stormed the Attica State Prison in New York, ending a five-day riot by about 1,200 inmates. Forty-three people, including nine guards held as hostages, were killed in the most devastating prison uprising in U.S. history. Most of the slain prisoners were black.

The troubles at Attica began with a misunderstanding between two inmates—one black and one white—who were playing touch football and a guard who thought they were fighting. Rumors then spread through the prison that guards had beaten the inmates, and the riot erupted. Other factors that helped spark the violence included growing black and Puerto Rican militancy among some inmates and poor prison conditions.

October 15. Elton Hayes, a seventeen-year-old black youth, was killed by police officers in Memphis, Tennessee. Five days of racial violence followed. Nine local law enforcement officers, including a black police lieutenant, were later charged with murder in the brutal death of the youth.

October. President Richard Nixon nominated William Rehnquist of Phoenix, Arizona, and Lewis F. Powell of Richmond, Virginia, to the U.S. Supreme Court. They were supposed to replace two associate justices who had recently retired, Hugo L. Black (who died just a little over a week after leaving the Court) and John M. Harlan.

Many blacks opposed both Rehnquist and Powell because they felt the two men had shown anti-black attitudes in their personal as well as their public lives. The U.S. Senate later confirmed both nominees without much difficulty.

December 15. Black Panther leader Huey Newton was declared a free man after a judge dropped manslaughter charges against him.

It was the third time Newton had been tried for the 1967 killing of a policeman in Oakland, California. His first trial ended in a conviction, but the conviction was later overturned. In the second and third trials, jurors were unable to reach a verdict. (Also see entries dated September 8, 1968; May 29, 1970; August, 1970; August 8, 1971; November 2, 1974; and August 22, 1989.)

December. Arthur B. Spingarn, a veteran champion of black rights, died at his home in New York at the age of ninety-three. A white civil rights lawyer, he had served as the NAACP's president since 1940 and also once headed its National Legal Committee. The organization's annual award of merit, the Spingarn Medal, was named in his honor.

1972

January 25. Shirley Chisholm, the first black woman to serve in the U.S. Congress, made history once again when she announced her intention to seek the Democratic presidential nomination. She was the first black and the first woman to do so.

January 27. Mahalia Jackson, one of the world's leading gospel singers, died at age sixty in Evergreen Park, Illinois. Known for her rich and powerful voice, she helped popularize gospel music by spreading it from black churches in the Deep South to concert halls throughout the world.

Jackson was born in 1911 in New Orleans, Louisiana. When she was sixteen, she moved to Chicago, Illinois and saved enough money from her job as a hotel maid to open a beauty shop. She also joined a local gospel choir.

Jackson made her first recording in 1934, but she did not become nationally famous until 1946. That year, she recorded "Move On Up a Little Higher," which sold over a million copies. She then toured around the world, at first enjoying even greater success in Europe than in America.

It was during the 1950s that Jackson finally became a star in her native country with hits such as "He's Got the Whole World in His Hands" and "When I Wake Up in Glory." She gave numerous concerts and also sang on radio and television programs. (Because of her religious beliefs, however, she refused to appear in nightclubs.) Jackson was also very active in the civil rights movement during the 1960s.

April 4. Adam Clayton Powell, Jr., U.S. Representative from Harlem for more than twenty years and one-time chairman of the influential House Education and Labor Committee, died at the age of sixty-three in Miami, Florida. (See entry dated August 1, 1944.)

Powell was surrounded with controversy in death as he had been in life. Two different women fought over his funeral arrangements and his estate. Finally, on April 10, his body was cremated and the ashes scattered over the island of Bimini in the Bahamas, a favorite vacation spot of Powell's.

June 4. In California, a jury acquitted black revolutionary Angela Davis on all charges of murder, kidnapping, and conspiracy stemming from a 1970 courtroom shooting that left a judge and three other men dead.

The shooting had occurred when three black convicts (including the so-called "Soledad Brothers") tried to escape while on trial for killing a prison guard at California's Soledad Prison. (See entry dated August 7, 1970.) Because of its strong political overtones, Davis's case had attracted attention from black and white liberals all over the world who wanted to make sure that she received a fair trial.

Just a couple of months before the jury announced its decision in the Davis case, an all-white jury in San Francisco had found the Soledad Brothers—Fleeta Drumgo and John Cluchette—innocent of killing the guard at Soledad Prison. The third convict who had been involved in the courtroom incident, George Jackson, died of a gunshot wound in prison in 1971. (Various reports claimed that he had been Davis's boyfriend.)

Once she was free, Davis resumed teaching and writing. She has also remained politically active. In late 1972, for example, she announced plans to form a national defense organization to provide legal aid to the "black and brown political prisoners of the government." In addition, Davis ran for vice-president on the Communist party's ticket in the 1980 and 1984 elections. (Also see entries dated October 13, 1970, and January 5, 1971.)

July 6. James E. Baker, a career black foreign service officer, was named economic and commercial officer at the U.S. embassy in Pretoria, South Africa. This made him the first black American diplomat to have a permanent assignment in a nation known for its strict policy of apartheid, or racial segregation.

July 12. South Dakota senator George McGovern won the Democratic presidential nomination at the party's convention in Miami Beach, Florida.

Representative Shirley Chisholm, the first black and the first woman to seek the nomination, had managed to gain the support of only a handful of delegates during the campaign. The Congressional Black Caucus had refused to back her, and she did not do well in the primaries. As a result, she could never successfully challenge McGovern.

November 2. Racial tensions flared in Lavonia, Georgia, after a black man was slain in a gun battle with police who said he opened fire on them as they tried to serve a warrant at his home. One policeman was wounded in the exchange of gunfire. Blacks insisted that the killing could have been avoided and almost immediately launched a boycott against downtown merchants in protest.

November 7. Richard Nixon was reelected president of the United States by one of the largest majorities in the nation's history. As had been the case in 1968, he failed to win much support from black voters. Instead, they chose his opponent, George McGovern.

November 16. Two black students at Southern University in Baton Rouge, Louisiana (one of the country's largest all-black colleges), were killed during a confrontation between black students and law enforcement officers. After the incident, police officials denied that their men had fired the fatal shots. Some suggested that the gunfire might have been accidental, but spokespersons for the students charged that the police had fired on purpose.

The Louisiana state government put together a biracial committee consisting of police officers, university administrators, students, elected officials, and private citizens to investigate the shootings. Some blacks did not trust the official committee, however. They promised to assemble a group of their own to look into the incident.

December 7. W. Sterling Cary, the administrative officer for about ninety United Church of Christ congregations in New York City, was unanimously elected president of the National Council of Churches at the group's annual meeting in Dallas, Texas.

The first black American to head the Council, Cary had served as a minister for twenty-four years. He was originally a Baptist pastor before he began preaching at Presbyterian, Congregational, and interdenominational churches.

December 15. Fifty special sheriff's deputies and police officers patrolled the Escambra High School in Pensacola, Florida, after a day of fighting between black and white students left several people injured.

Index